The Entrepreneurial Effect: Waterloo

INVENIRE BOOKS

Invenire Books is an Ottawa-based "idea factory" specializing in collaborative governance and stewardship. Invenire and its authors offer creative and practical responses to the challenges and opportunities faced by today's complex organizations.

Invenire Books welcomes a range of contributions – from conceptual and theoretical reflections, ethnographic and case studies, and proceedings of conferences and symposia, to works of a very practical nature – that deal with problems or issues on the governance and stewardship front. Invenire Books publishes works in French and English.

This is the sixth volume published by Invenire Books.

INVENIRE is associated with the Centre on Governance of the University of Ottawa, and also collaborates to publish a quarterly electronic journal www.optimumonline.ca that reaches more than 10,000 subscribers.

The titles published by Invenire Books are listed at the end of this book.

The Entrepreneurial Effect: Waterloo

*Practical Advice from your own
Virtual Board of Advisors*

Selected by

James Bowen

Invenire Books
Ottawa, Canada

2011

Cover Blackberry photo courtesy of Ross Cheriton

Photos of the contributors, selecting editor and various entrepreneurs are courtesy of the contributors. In some cases, photos of the entrepreneur-authors were not received or were received too late for inclusion.

Library and Archives Canada Cataloguing in Publication

The entrepreneurial effect : Waterloo : practical advice from your own virtual board of advisors / selected by James Bowen.

Includes index.
Issued also in electronic format.
ISBN 978-0-9813931-9-3

1. New business enterprises--Ontario--Waterloo. 2. Business planning--Ontario--Waterloo. 3. Entrepreneurship--Ontario-- Waterloo. 4. Business incubators--Ontario--Waterloo. I. Bowen, James, 1962-

HD62.5.E582 2011   658.1'1   C2011-904714-4

ISBN 978-0-9813931-9-3 (print)   Ebook: 978-0-9868716-0-3

Published by Invenire Books, an imprint of Invenire,
PO Box 87001
Ottawa, Canada K2P 1X0
www.invenire.ca

Designed and Printed in Canada by Cheriton Graphics
Distributed by:
Commoners' Publishing
631 Tubman Cr. Ottawa, Canada K1V 8L6
Tel: (613) 523-2444 fax: (613) 260-0401
sales@commonerspublishing.com
www.commonerspublishing.com

Contents

List of Sponsors and Ads

Biographies of Authors

List of Figures and Tables

Acknowledgments

This book wouldn't have been possible without the contributions of many people.

I would like to start with Dr. Feridun Hamdullahpur, President of the University of Waterloo, who immediately accepted to do the foreword.

The book started with the support of Thom Ryan at Communitech in Waterloo who helped scope out the original list of contributors, which brings us to the contributors themselves. These people have a great deal of experience and expertise and are willing to give back to the community.

We also need to mention Iain Klug and (again) Thom Ryan of Communitech for their early support to the project. As well, we note Howard Armitage, former Executive Director Conrad Center for Business, Entrepreneurship and Technology at the University of Waterloo, and Steve Farlow Executive Director, Schlegel Centre for Entrepreneurship at Wilfrid Laurier University, and, Rod B. McNaughton Director Conrad Center for Business, Entrepreneurship and Technology at the University of Waterloo for their support and help finding contributors.

I also want to note that Ted Hastings was the first to have his article submitted.

I would like to note the following individuals who understood the value of supporting the technology community: Mike Gassewitz, Steve Farlow, Denny Doyle, Peter Sommerer and Rod B. McNaughton.

I would also like to acknowledge Sacha DeGroot and Janet Ross of Sandvine, Lori Nave and Beverly Desousa of NexJSystems, Valerie Beyer of Desire2Learn, Brandon Sweet of the University of Waterloo and Stephen Rahal of Igloo software for their efforts on keeping some of the articles on track.

Finally we need to acknowledge the support of Glenn Cheriton for his great help in the editorial process, and of Ruth Hubbard and Gilles Paquet of the publisher Invenire Books.

FOREWORD

Feridun Hamdullahpur

When I was invited to contribute the foreword to this book, I hesitated for a moment or two before replying in the affirmative. After all, why would a university president be asked to write the foreword for a book celebrating entrepreneurship?

When one is lucky enough to be serving as president of the University of Waterloo, the answer is quite clear. I was asked because entrepreneurship is embedded in the DNA of this university's staff, faculty, and students. And, that, as the poet Robert Frost so eloquently put it, has made all the difference.

The phrase "knowledge economy" has been widely used in recent years to describe how societies can be built around the effective use of knowledge. There is a worldwide aspiration to link culture, the environment, health, technology, and innovation, and use those links to advance both society and the economy for the benefit of all. A knowledge economy is one that views knowledge as a resource, valued not only for its own sake, but also as the key ingredient in social and economic productivity.

What role do universities and other institutions of higher learning play in the knowledge economy? We supply knowledge-creating, talented human capital to the regions in which our institutions reside, and, more importantly, to the global economy. I believe innovation is the natural pipeline between universities and the broader world outside them.

Waterloo Region is a thriving example of a knowledge economy. *The Globe and Mail* describes Waterloo as a place "in which talent, industry, and post-secondary schools feed off one another's energy and ideas to grow ever more innovative and prosperous."

Waterloo Region is now known widely for its high-tech cluster, but, as the *Globe and Mail* reported in late 2010, the University of Waterloo is "the cornerstone of the region's cluster. From its beginnings in 1957, when it was created to train engineers and technicians, it allowed professors and graduate students to keep all the revenues from the commercial use of their research." The result, says William Elliot, business development manager of Canada's Technology Triangle, also quoted in the *Globe*: "You have these entrepreneurial professors and students working on new projects, and developing spinoff companies."

Waterloo Region has a long tradition of adding value. Its enterprising 19th century settlers built distilleries, mills, tanneries, and factories, making use of the abundant raw materials already present in the community. The region developed a diversified economy of agriculture, manufacturing, and export.

In the 21st century, our diversified economy is still here, but knowledge has become the No. 1 renewable resource in our community. The buildings that once housed distilleries, warehouses, and tanneries are now occupied by think tanks, high-tech start-ups, and talented workers. Waterloo excels in attracting, retaining, and training skilled entrepreneurs, whose ideas become innovations.

Entrepreneurial Effect: Waterloo is a clearinghouse of collected wisdom from some of the most successful graduates of Waterloo's entrepreneurial culture. In the following pages, you will read about some of the fantastic stories and lessons learned by some of our most prominent innovators.

Many of this book's contributors have strong links to Waterloo Region's post-secondary institutions, including the University of Waterloo. This should come as no surprise. Waterloo is committed to experiential learning and co-operative education. We have established programs and activities such as the Conrad Centre for Business, Entrepreneurship and Technology and its Master of Business, Entrepreneurship, and Technology program. We founded VeloCity, a student innovation "dormcubator" where some of our brightest and most motivated students can access industry expertise. VeloCity is growing beyond the residence building where it started: there are now summer boot camps and start-up space at the Communitech Hub in downtown Kitchener. As well, Waterloo offers business and entrepreneurship programs in every faculty, weaving together study of a discipline such as science or environment with courses and experience in business.

Our open intellectual property policy has helped lay the groundwork for the smooth transfer of ideas from the laboratory and the lecture hall to the marketplace. We foster global citizens by educating our students with the world in mind, while at the same time attracting the brightest minds from abroad to study at our campuses. That builds a critical mass of world-changing ideas right here at home.

This university, however, would not be where it is today without the community that built us, and infused our students, faculty, and staff with the same spirit of entrepreneurship that has existed since the 19th century. Local industry – the manufacturing giants of the mid-20th century – were crucial in shaping our fledgling university's academic programs and getting our unique co-operative education system off the ground, as were the insurance companies which encouraged us to offer co-operative education programs outside of the engineering discipline in the mid 1960s, starting a trend that has seen us expand experiential learning opportunities to all six of our faculties. We have also benefited time and again from the vision of inspired leaders from the municipal, regional, provincial, and federal governments.

The University of Waterloo is proud of the role it plays in the Waterloo Region's entrepreneurial environment, and our association with Waterloo's brightest entrepreneurial minds. For more than 53 years, this university has sought to maintain the highest academic standards of teaching, learning, and research, while making all three relevant to the wider world. Supporting the drive to use knowledge to create innovative ideas is the core of our mission.

What are the fruits of our community's efforts? More than 700 high-tech businesses now operate in the region. We are home to a thriving arts and cultural sector, with museums, galleries, and theatres. Urban renewal has breathed new life into old neighbourhoods.

At the Accelerator Centre in our Research and Technology Park, and at the Communitech Hub in downtown Kitchener, established players have the opportunity to rub shoulders with, and mentor the next generation of start-up ventures. In Waterloo, we are celebrating knowledge in all its forms.

Is it any wonder that the Bank of Montreal has referred to Waterloo Region as "one of the brightest stars in the Canadian economic skies"? However, it's more accurate to say that we aren't just one star; we are a constellation. Waterloo Region is distinguishing itself as a cluster for the production and utilization of the very kind of talented human capital that will make or break Canada's position in the knowledge economy. I invite you to read on, and find new ways to make knowledge the key to your success.

Feridun Hamdullahpur, President, University of Waterloo

Feridun Hamdullahpur is currently the President at the University of Waterloo. He was appointed Provost and Vice-President (Academic) at the University of Waterloo in September 2009. He is a Professor of Mechanical and Mechatronics Engineering at UW. His teaching and research interests are in the areas of thermo-fluids and energy conversion systems.

Before coming to Waterloo, Dr. Hamdullahpur served as the Provost and Vice President Academic (2006-2009) and as the Vice President

Research and International (2000-2006) at Carleton University in Ottawa. Prior to his move to Carleton, he was the Associate Principal, Graduate Studies and Research at DalTech, Dalhousie University (1997-2000). He was Associate Dean of Graduate Studies (1993-95), and Dean of Graduate Studies and Research (1995-97). In these various positions, his mandate was to provide leadership in developing new academic and research initiatives, and in integrating research, graduate studies, technology-knowledge transfer and international programs and expertise, as well as to liaise with government, business, granting councils, other universities and organizations on research and academic matters.

Dr. Hamdullahpur received his Bachelor's and Master's degrees in Mechanical Engineering at the Technical University of Istanbul, Turkey, and a Ph.D. in Chemical Engineering at the Technical University of Nova Scotia in Halifax, Canada.

Dr. Hamdullahpur has been an active researcher and supervisor. His research areas include energy conversion, thermo-fluids and bio-mass gasification and combustion. He has published over 130 scientific and technical articles and supervised over 40 graduate students.

Introduction

James Bowen

This is the second book in the "Entrepreneurial Effect" series. It deals with some of the many entrepreneurs linked with the Waterloo, Canada area. Entrepreneurs of this area have "punched above their weight" on the world business stage, indeed, many have suggested that there is "something in the water" (or DNA) of the region which drives that success. We explore what that "something" might be in this book.

The divisions of this book, into "lessons in entrepreneurship", "market, product, sales, people" (some may think of this as managing), and "making it happen" suggest three keys to the success of Waterloo entrepreneurs. It is clear that the entrepreneurs in this book are doing a lot right, and are willing to share their experiences.

Perhaps the "entrepreneurial community" of Waterloo has taken tech entrepreneurship more seriously than other communities. It can be argued that there is no magic in educational and technological grounding, being good at the mechanics of business, and making it happen. While true, this misses the team psychology of Waterloo in systematically developing entrepreneurs for world class success. One can deconstruct entrepreneurship to explain away success but the Waterloo experience suggests that the methods of the Waterloo Region and their entrepreneurs can be copied and adapted by other communities, companies and entrepreneurs, with improved chances of success.

Entrepreneurial Effect Contradictions

One of the ironies of entrepreneurialism is that whatever is said, generally the opposite can also seem just as valid:
- Entrepreneurs are all different yet have similar characteristics.
- Entrepreneurs follow disciplined methods, yet leap into the unknown with "out of the box" thinking.
- Entrepreneurs take risks, yet manage to reduce risk.
- Entrepreneurialism is an art, but also a science.
- An entrepreneur must be a leader; an entrepreneur must be a team player.
- Entrepreneurs are both selfless and selfish.

Learning about, practicing and being an entrepreneur sometimes seems keeping these contradictions in mind and acting on them, without being paralyzed by them.

The Origin of the "Entrepreneurial Effect"

Many years ago, as a young entrepreneur I often made decisions with not enough information, a lot of uncertainty and little experience. As many others have and continue to do, I recognized that I needed to continue to increase my abilities to understand the big picture, make decisions and "make it happen".

Over the years I sought out sources that could provide me with the knowledge that I needed to grow as a professional. Often I found abstract concepts or concepts taken from different fields had been twisted to make them seem applicable to the business of starting and growing technology-based product and service companies. I found words that sounded good but were unrealistic or had no accompanying guidance on how to make them applicable to my situation.

I searched for a better way to effect entrepreneurialism. This book is my response.

Starting Companies

To start and grow companies we need good, talented people with a passion for making a dream happen, a viable opportunity and mentors and advisors who have done it before. We need investors, founders, employees, customers, and partners, consultants who are willing to take a chance to see innovation happen. We need timeless ideas on how to succeed. We need people who seek out, recognize and act on opportunities.

Growing our Ability

Wisdom can be defined as the coordination of "knowledge and experience" and its deliberate use to improve well-being. In the preceding definition, we have three concepts: knowledge, experience and usability. It is the coupling of knowledge and experience and the ability to use it in a particular situation that is of value.

Let us not forget our old Greek friend, Aristotle, who defined wisdom as the knowledge of causes: *why* things exist in a particular fashion. That is what we are after in this book. Understanding cause and effect, why, what, and how.

In my travels and interactions with entrepreneurs, investors and others in the tech industry, the cry to improve and grow is loud and clear. This cry can be heard in seminars, newspaper columns and around the keyboards in offices across the technology community. And this cry is always loudest amongst the entrepreneurs themselves. We entrepreneurs recognize that the future is growing in complexity and we need to be ready. We often find ourselves making decisions outside of our area of expertise – something that is common for those concerned with starting and growing tech companies, When we step outside our comfort zone we can find ourselves in a different technology area than we are familiar with or making management decisions as a technology person and vice versa.

Whether it is in informal settings or formal meeting venues, we want to know:

• What should I do in this situation?
• Is what I am doing the right thing to do?

It's often validating that what we are doing is right, not just learning something new.

Sometimes the advice we seek from others is confirmation that what we have implemented is right, that it has been done by someone else and that it worked.

The need to get back to basics has become even more prevalent over the years as the tech industry matures and stabilizes. It is more difficult to find something new and make a company out of it. The room for mistakes is smaller.

As the room for mistakes shrinks, the need to hit the ground already in gear increases. Management can't have a long learning curve, the money isn't there and neither is the time. This book addresses these issues. It is a gathering of ideas that have worked; each author has provided the context in which their insights have worked and provided the reader with ideas that can go from paper to practice.

Who is the Book for?

It is for investors, advisor/mentors, founders, entrepreneurs, professional managers, inventors, consultants, academics, students and others interested in the start-up and growth of technology based product and service companies.

If you are not in a tech business...

While the lessons learned in this book come from the technology industry. I believe that the majority of ideas are applicable to any product company. So if you aren't in the tech industry, read the articles and perhaps the book will spark your imagination to adapt it to your industry and your situation. Most businesses are tech businesses in some way: the need to exploit the Internet, etc. Most business management skills (product, service, people, sales, etc) are similar in tech and "non-tech" businesses.

Learn for success

In this book, we have selected entrepreneurs because of their great ideas, their experience and examples they show. The fact that they have been successful in their chosen field helps validate their ideas. Inspirational stories are good reading but ideas that we can implement are what we want.

You don't need to read this book in a linear fashion, I suggest you seek out the articles of contributors whom you want to hear from or on topics that are plaguing you. If you are searching for specific content, please check the *Contents* page and the *Index* for direction and key points.

The book was not designed to be a one-time read and then shelf ware. It was designed for you to refer to and re-read whenever an issue/problem needs to be solved. There is great depth in most articles.

The last chapter is a test of your entrepreneurship skills.

Proceeds from this book

I want to thank you for buying this book, and want you to know that each of the contributors, including myself, are not making any money from this book.

The proceeds go to help support student entrepreneurs in the form of scholarships. This will help the tech industry to continue to grow and thrive.

The Contributors

Each of the contributors is writing because they want to give back to the tech community. I want to thank them for donating their time and effort to help make this happen. Thank you for supporting a good cause.

Along with each article is short biography of the contributor to give the reader a sense of context of the experience. By knowing something of their experience we learn something about the validity of the lesson.

Also included is a picture of the contributor so you if happen to see them in airport somewhere you can identify them and perhaps start a conversation about further lessons.

We are online at: www.entrepreneurialeffect.com You may contact me through the website or email me at jbowen@ces.on.ca with your comments about the book or the ideas presented herein.

James Bowen
Ottawa, Canada
June, 2011

PART I
LESSONS IN ENTREPRENEURSHIP

Canadian Innovation Centre

The Canadian Innovation Centre provides decision support to individuals, corporations and the government communities that support them, with the objective of significantly improving the rate of innovative product commercialization

Guiding innovation to be market-ready.
since 1975

Recognizing if you are an Entrepreneur

Robert Pavlis

One of the most important skills an entrepreneur can have is the ability to understand himself (read herself as appropriate throughout). I am not talking about writing up a glowing description of yourself. Understanding yourself means that you have the ability to look very deep inside yourself to really understand your wants, your needs, your strengths and most importantly your weaknesses.

Starting and running your own company will be one of the most exciting things you do in life. It is full of rewards both personal and financial. It is also full of problems, headaches, disappointments and a lot of hard work. In order for you to survive you will require certain tactical and emotional skills that most people do not possess.

Should you be an entrepreneur?

An entrepreneur in his first start-up company needs to wear many hats. It requires many operational skills such as sales, marketing, finance, people management; the list goes on. It also requires technical skills that are specific to your niche market.

An honest self-examination will reveal your strengths and weaknesses. With this knowledge you can then hire the skills you lack. The difficulty is being very honest with yourself.

Just as important is a requirement for what I will call emotional skills. Can you make decisions? Can you live with the risks? Can you look failure in the eye and see success around the corner? You can also hire for these skills, but if you plan to run a company you need to possess them yourself.

I meet with other business owners once a month and it seems that no matter how bad business gets, every one of them can see the good times just ahead. Next year is always going to be better than this year. This is a critical emotional skill to have.

Running a company is a very lonely job. You make the final decisions and you suffer the consequences. You need the emotional skills not only to handle such a situation, but to thrive in it. The ability to make tough decisions is one of the key differentiators between leaders and followers.

Risk

Running a business is all about taking risk. Every decision you make has an upside and a downside which translates into a degree of risk. It is important to understand your comfort level for risk and then make the decisions that have an acceptable risk level.

How much risk is the right amount of risk? There is no right answer. Some people risk everything including their home for a chance to be successful. Others limit their financial risk. Deciding on how much risk you are willing to take in your business is not that different from taking risk in the stock market. The important thing is that emotionally you are comfortable with the level of risk you take.

When I started my company I did it with virtually no cash. The only thing I risked was my full-time job. Through the years we have always financed growth from profits which means no outside investors and no banks to worry about. The consequence of this decision is that I maintain a low level of financial risk. It also means that the company grew slower than it could have. It is a balance that lets me sleep at night.

Are you an engineer?

Most technology companies start with a great idea which engineers turn into a product. Once the product exists, the company has to develop an ability for sales, marketing, and operations. The reality is that there are very few people who are good at both engineering and business and this can cause real problems in a start-up technology company.

If the owner is an engineer, the company makes great products that may never sell. If the owner is great at business there may never be great products.

It is critical that you evaluate your skills and your emotional desires to see what role best suits you. Even a small technology company needs both an engineer and a business person.

When I look back at the history of our company, it is clear to me that we spent the first dozen years being an engineering company. We made great products and sold enough to grow the company but we never ran the company as a real business. Why did we do this? I really like inventing new things – it is that simple. I have business skills, but my emotional desires lie on the engineering side of the business.

It is important to understand that there is nothing wrong with running an engineering company as long as you develop enough business to pay the bills. What is important is that you understand yourself, and your goals.

Companies mature

In many ways companies are like people; they grow and they change. There are tremendous differences between a company with 5 people and one with 50 people. With a small number of people, everyone knows everything and there is virtually no need for processes. As the company grows the requirement for process increases. Does your personality allow you to work in a more structured environment? Do you have the skills to develop a more structured environment? Many entrepreneurs don't and it is one reason businesses fail to grow.

As a company grows the culture of the company usually changes as well. Things become more formal. New levels of management develop which tends to create an "us versus them" attitude among some people. As the culture of the company changes you will have to change as well. It is important that you separate yourself from being "one of the gang". As more people join the company you need to be seen more and more as a leader. You need to mature along with the company.

Companies also go through a maturation process. In our case we started selling to smaller companies in less regulated environments. This made sense since the customer was more like us, also a small company, and meeting their requirements was easier. Over time we wanted to play with the big boys. We wanted to sell to Fortune 500 pharmaceutical companies but that was not going to happen without some drastic changes. We reinvented the products and our whole sales process. We started meeting more regulatory requirements, and we even moved so that we had a higher quality office.

As a leader your skill set will need to change. The requirements of the business may not line up well with your personal desires and you need to make some important decisions. It is important you understand your new role before you start the change process and you need to be willing to take on the risk of change.

Growth also changes the requirements for your management team. Managing a department of two people is quite different from managing 12. Many managers can't grow with the company and at some point you will outgrow many of your managers. Are you willing and able to replace old time friends when the need arises? Will you decide against this and keep the company small? There is no right answer but it is important that your decisions match your personality and your personal priorities.

Time to step aside

It is rare to find an individual who is good at running a small company and a large one. At some point you will likely be the road block to your company's growth. How will you handle this? Are you willing and able to step aside and let someone else run your show? Do you have the mental skills to embrace this and allow it to happen? These are not typical entrepreneurial skills. We entrepreneurs like to be in charge and we certainly don't like to be told what to do.

There is more to life than work

I am an avid white water canoeist and kayaker. About 8 years ago I was asked to join a group for a month-long trip in central Labrador. I really wanted to go but I couldn't because I could not leave the business for such a long period of time. There is no cell coverage in central Labrador. For many months I regretted my decision.

The following year I decided to go on a 2 week solo canoe trip in the Yukon. When I got back I was caught up on my work in less than 7 hours. The following year it was a 4 week trip to the Arctic and again when I returned I was caught up in about 7 hours.

I learned an important lesson. When I am not around, people do not come to me for help. Instead they solve their own problems. That is good for me, good for my employees and very good for the growth of my company.

I am a rare breed in that I do not carry a cell phone or a Blackberry. If I am not in the office I am either busy working somewhere else or I am taking time off work. In either case I don't want to be disturbed.

Be true to yourself

The above are just some of the reasons you should spend time understanding yourself. The challenge now is to use this information to make better decisions. Should you start a business? What role will you take in the business? What is a successful business for *you*?

There are no right and wrong answers here. The most important thing is that you are true to yourself. Follow your own heart and do things in a way that makes you feel good. You will be making the right decisions if they match your personality and your personal goals.

Know yourself. It will help you make the right decisions.

Robert Pavlis

I was born in Vienna and moved to Canada as a young child. After graduating with an M.Sc. in Biochemistry (Guelph and Western) and a science/math teaching certificate I landed a job working for an American company selling laboratory equipment in Canada. As the only Canadian employee I had to learn how to handle everything related to sales, support and office operations. A year later I was hired by a small Edmonton-based company, Terrochem Laboratories to open an office in Eastern Canada and became their VP of sales and operations.

After 8 years I was convinced I knew more than my supervisors and I decided to start my own business, Labtronics Inc. In 1986 I started Labtronics Inc to provide software automation solutions for analytical laboratories. This company has been instrumental in bringing many new informatics inventions to the market place. The most significant development was the introduction of *LimsLink*, the first commercial product to interface instruments to Laboratory Information Management Systems and we remain the global leader in this niche market. We are currently in the process of completely changing the way labs are automated. Instead of separate isolated software systems we are spearheading the way towards a single informatics system to automate the whole lab, called an *iLAB*, for integrated lab.

I still find it amazing that someone with limited experience can end up producing products that affect millions of people every day.

Lessons for Entrepreneurs

Dan Mathers

So you want to be an entrepreneur? There's a lot to learn for first time entrepreneurs, and a lot to learn for second time entrepreneurs, and a lot to learn for third time entrepreneurs! A quest for constant learning is a key trait in successful entrepreneurs. I thought that what might be helpful is to discuss the what, when, why, how and where of learning for entrepreneurs.

Lessons in the "what"…

One of the significant differences between taking a role in a large company and starting your own entrepreneurial venture is that when you are an entrepreneur, particularly when you are first starting out, you need to do everything yourself, or with a very small team. If you're starting a technology business, chances are you understand the technology that is core to your business, but perhaps you've never been exposed to effective product development processes, or how to ensure that your product platform scales effectively. Maybe you understand all of this stuff, but what you're missing is knowledge about product management, or how to select the right product features at the right price to optimize your value proposition. Maybe you need to learn how to do competitive analysis, or how to build a financial model, or how to raise investment capital, how to put together a go-to-market strategy, do a distribution agreement, develop an IP strategy, put proper corporate governance in place, how to develop a strategic partner relationship and so on. The point is, that at every step of the evolution of your business there is a lot to learn, and in all likelihood getting this knowledge will help you avoid mistakes and help you accelerate the growth of your business.

"When" is the right time to learn all of this?

Many successful entrepreneurs will tell you that they are learning all the time. The best way to get this training is by doing. In other words, there is no better way than learning what you need to do on an as-needed basis. You encounter an issue, and you find a way to go out and solve it. As your knowledge base expands, you catalogue these learning points, and so you come up the learning curve, with ever more new and different challenges to solve, but now you have a solid base of past problems solved to use in problem solving. I think that's one of the things that experienced entrepreneurs learn: there are no new problems to solve, just different contexts within which the problem must be solved. So when is the best time to start learning to be an entrepreneur? Now, with every step you take.

"Why" you need to learn...

The truth is, you don't. That's right, you don't need to learn all of this stuff. Lots of people get by with big gaps in their knowledge base on the conventional wisdom of how to be a successful entrepreneur. Sometimes, an entrepreneur just inherently understands what needs to be done and manages to do it well. Sometimes, an entrepreneur has the foresight to build a team around him or her with people who have the requisite skills. And sometimes an entrepreneur just gets lucky. Being at the right place, at the right time, with the right product idea and the right story counts for a lot. Having all of the knowledge in the world without luck on your side means that it is a much tougher road to success.

There are many ways to succeed, however, consider this: Building a successful entrepreneurial venture is a very risky endeavour. You need and want to give yourself every edge possible, and learning as many of the requisite skills of how to be a successful entrepreneur as possible will help give you that edge.

"How" do you go about learning to be an entrepreneur?

The good news is that there are many, many people who want to help, and many ways to get help. Learning how to be a successful entrepreneur may be an ongoing endeavour, but you can set yourself up for success by getting a good grounding in the basics. If you're currently in school, you'll probably know that there are many excellent courses on entrepreneurship, starting at the high school level, as well as at the undergraduate and graduate level. At Wilfrid Laurier University, the Schlegel Centre for Business and Entrepreneurship provides a solid grounding in developing Entrepreneurial skills. The MBET (Master of Business, Entrepreneurship and Technology) at the University of Waterloo is also an excellent program. But what if you aren't a student and don't wish to go back to school? Well, there are many other ways that you can get help. One of the great things about Waterloo Region is that collaboration is built into the DNA of the region.

I've lived and worked in each of the three points of the Ontario technology triangle: Toronto, Ottawa and Waterloo. Ontario, and specifically each of these regions, are all amazing places to build a technology business. More recently, I've been fortunate to have spent a lot of time in Waterloo Region, and it is indeed a very special place. The special nature of Waterloo Region has a lot to do with the ecosystem.

In Waterloo Region, the ecosystem is alive and well, and is a key reason why the technology businesses in the region are thriving. I've never seen a region where industry, the universities, government, professional service firms, the regional support organizations like the Accelerator Centre, MARS, Communitech, the Ontario Centres of Excellence, DFAIT, IRAP, all of the other organizations with a regional presence, the MaRS Investment Accelerator Fund and angel investors all work so well together to help entrepreneurs build successful businesses. There are many reasons, including the combination of our regional culture, our size and scale, and our close integration as a community working hard to grow and expand our entrepreneurial successes.

From my vantage point, I see many individuals with a passion for seeing this region be successful, and this is definitely a case where success breeds success. This is now built into our regional DNA, and will continue to contribute to our success for many years to come. I'm sure you're asking why I'm telling you all of this, aside from providing a pretty blatant endorsement of the region. I'm telling you this because this is precisely where the help lies.

So you're an entrepreneur wanting to get help? Get engaged in the community. A great way to do this is by becoming a member of Communitech, and attending some of the excellent networking events and Peer to Peer groups that they organize and host. You need office space? Consider starting your business at one of the two facilities run by the Accelerator Centre: the Accelerator Centre in Waterloo, or the Digital Media HUB in Kitchener. These are world class facilities that have a stable of in-house mentors that is second to none when it comes to providing real world advice to entrepreneurs, and it's included in your rent!

But what if your business is located elsewhere in the region? Don't despair. First of all, MaRS has created the Entrepreneur's Toolkit, which is a large collection of tools to help you build your business. All of the materials can be accessed on their website www.marsdd.com. In addition, the Venture Services group, part of the Ontario Networks of Excellence, is there to provide advice and counsel to companies both at the Accelerator Centre and the Digital Media HUB. The Venture Services group is comprised of experienced, serial entrepreneurs and has been in existence for several years now. These serial entrepreneurs are there to help with every aspect of building your business, and really act with no other agenda than helping you build a successful start-up technology company in the region. There are no fees charged for this help. All that is required is that you are a technology start-up looking for coaching and mentorship.

In addition to getting help from these excellent sources, there are many angel investors in the region willing to help, as well as angel organizations like the Golden Triangle Angels. They are, of course, very interested in investing in successful start-ups, but I've found that these individuals are also the source for some great help and coaching in the region.

Another great source of help is the Investment Accelerator Fund, a part of the Ontario Networks of Excellence. The fund invests in early stage technology start-ups. I'm an Investment Director for the fund, and handle the deal flow for Southwestern Ontario. The fund is not only a great potential source for investment capital, but it is also a great potential source of coaching and mentorship. If you'd like to find out more, including whether your start-up fits the fund's investment profile, please give me a call or send me an email.

I've really only scratched the surface here. There are many additional sources of help. Any one of the places above is a great place to start.

The final question: "where" to learn all of this...

Right here in Waterloo of course! Waterloo Region is a really great place to build a start-up right now. There has never been a better time, with more support and funding available than any time in recent memory.

The help is there. You just have to decide you're going to take it.

Dan Mathers

Dan is President & CEO, IronBit Inc.

Dan has 25 years of experience leading technology businesses, and has led all sizes of businesses from large divisions of multi-nationals, to involvement as founder and member of the leadership team for multiple successful start-ups. These businesses have created more than $1 billion in shareholder value.

Currently, Dan is the IAF Investment Director for Southwestern Ontario, and is responsible for driving all of the investments in the region. He is also a part of the executive team at P&P Optica, a very promising growth company in Waterloo Region.

In addition, Dan is currently a member of the Boards of Directors for several for-profit and not-for-profit organizations.

Entrepreneurs and Creativity

Robert Tong

I have met successful entrepreneurs who know entrepreneurism runs in their blood and that they are "born" to create and start new businesses. These are the lucky few. The majority of others, like me, occasionally wonder whether we have what it takes to be a successful entrepreneur.

I can't remember exactly when it was back in the late 1980s when I asked myself that exact question. At the time, I was getting restless as a mid-level manager in mid-sized company - COM DEV Ltd.- and wondered whether I could ever leave the corporate world and start a business of my own. So, I researched entrepreneurism to look for materials and tools that would help me assess my entrepreneurial potential. That was in pre-Google days and researching any topic was a considerably more tedious process. Nevertheless, I did land on a simple evaluation tool that assesses a person's entrepreneurial potential based on 10 attributes.

I can no longer remember what all those 10 attributes are, but I do remember that I was devastated by the assessment outcome. I scored as low as anyone could in terms of having any potential to be an entrepreneur. If the assessment is accurate, I should give up any hope of ever becoming an entrepreneur and just simply stick to my day job.

I do remember three of the 10 attributes because I was so far off the scale on each one in the wrong direction. In no particular order, they are

Whether I did well in school;

Whether I am creative; and

Whether I am a risk taker.

Apparently, the better one does in school, the less likely he or she would be an entrepreneur. Since I always did very well in university, the conclusion is that I am not likely going to be an entrepreneur based on this attribute. After all, both Bill Gates and Mike Lazaridis didn't even graduate from university. Apparently, entrepreneurs are typically so consumed by their desire and drive to create new business ideas that they never bother with grades in school.

I never thought I was a creative person because I was an engineer. I saw myself as skilled in solving problems but not creative. Since I didn't think creativity was something that can be learned, the low score in this attribute dealt me a big blow.

I also judged myself very risk adverse, which again suggested that I don't have what it takes to be an entrepreneur. This was the other big blow to my hope of ever becoming an entrepreneur because again I didn't think the capacity for risk taking is something that can be "learned."

I don't remember the other seven attributes because I believe those related to things that can be learned or changed. It was these three that I believed there was nothing I could do anything about, and I was right at the bottom end of the scale in all three of them.

I am writing this today because someone thought I have proven myself to be a successful entrepreneur. Indeed, I have now even convinced myself that I have what it takes to be an entrepreneur. So, what changed?

I am not going to bother with the "did well in school" thing because I now simply believe the author of the assessment tool at the time was simply misguided. It takes just as much focus, discipline, intelligence and hard work to do well in school as it does to be a successful entrepreneur. People like Bill Gates and Mike Lazaridis could easily have done exceptionally well in school if they chose to. They were simply more focused on their businesses at the time. I, on the other hand, was more focused on school when I was in school.

I thought I wasn't creative simply because I was naïve and had a narrow view of creativity at that time. Now that I have a few more years behind me, I could see that I am actually quite a "creative" problem solver. Creativity comes in different forms, and I am certainly not lacking in creativity in areas that are important to starting and growing a business. So, I probably misjudged myself in this attribute at the time. I am glad that I found out I do have creativity after all.

The one attribute I do want to talk more about is the one on "risk taking." This is because I did know for a fact that I was very risk adverse, and few would argue that entrepreneurs are risk takers.

Not long before taking this entrepreneurial potential assessment, I was involved in a personal development training program where I happened to have uncovered my high degree of risk aversion in one of the exercises. The bottom line was that I nearly panicked when I discovered during the exercise that I had a one in a hundred chance of failing. Of course I didn't fail because the odds were so much in my favour. However, I distinctly remembered telling myself that I really have no capacity to take any risks if I would panic over a one-in-a-hundred chance of failing. That was the reason why I gave myself a "zero" in risk taking capacity.

Despite the abysmal score from the assessment, for some reason I wasn't willing to give up. I set myself a 10-year goal to become an entrepreneur. How I came up with that figure, I didn't know, but I figure I would need at least that much time given how poorly I scored. The aspect I focused on was on the risk taking capacity. I figured that if I could get that one worked out and surround myself with others who could make up for what I lacked in the other attributes, perhaps I could still give entrepreneurism a go. I also went on to do an MBA in 1993 to round out some of the skills I believed I'd need.

To figure out this risk capacity thing, I took every opportunity I had to talk to successful entrepreneurs to understand why they possess this greater capacity to take risks. It didn't take me long to find out that these entrepreneurs are not the "risk junkies" I thought they would be. In fact, in one of these conversations I had with Val O'Donovan, founder of COM DEV International, he told me he is not a risk taker at all. He likes to see that he has a 60% to 70% chance of success before he undertakes an investment in a new business initiative. What became rapidly clear to me was that these entrepreneurs take only "calculated risks." More importantly, they approach risks in an analytical and intellectual manner. What they don't do is react to risk in an emotional way the way that I did. While I get consumed by the downside of failing, they weigh the benefits of winning against the downside of losing analytically. They gladly take on the risks once they are convinced that the benefits of winning outweighs the downside of losing, that they can live with the downside of losing and the probability of winning is acceptable for the upside and downside involved.

Once I got that concept through my thick skull, I was on my way to take my first big step into entrepreneurism. That involved overcoming the fear to quit my well paying job to go do something new. Applying the newly acquired insight, I came to the following conclusion:

The unemployment rate at the time was only 10%. Since I was a good performer (at least top quartile), the probability of not being able to find another job if I needed to was pretty low;

The worst case of quitting was that I might get a lower paying job and I might have to relocate for the position, which would have been both unpleasant but acceptable outcomes; but I would hate to be filled with regret when I am old and retired that I had not given something new a try.

The irrational fear of quitting did not immediately go away despite having done the risk analysis intellectually. Moments of panic still crept in over the days leading up to my final resignation. I had to remind myself each time not to let emotion take control of my logical decision.

Over the years as I rode the entrepreneur journey, whether I was involved in a start-up or a new business venture in a corporation, the application of the above has gotten easier and the "fear of failure" has become no more than just an additional gut check.

You could say I am in the firm camp in which I believe you make who you want to be. You can become an entrepreneur if you want to.

Robert Tong

Robert Tong serves as vice president of ON Semiconductor's medical division. With more than two decades of experience in high-tech companies, Robert oversees the division's product development and customer relationship management. He was previously senior vice president of the medical business unit of AMI Semiconductor.

From 2000 to 2004, Robert served as President and CEO of Dspfactory, a successful start-up company acquired by AMI. While with Dspfactory, Robert was instrumental in signing customer agreements with the top digital hearing-aid manufactures around the world and leading Dspfactory to become the number one DSP standard product supplier. Recognized for technical innovation and global expansion under his leadership, he also successfully expanded the company's product line into new markets.

Prior to Dspfactory, Robert served as senior vice president of the space products business unit at COM DEV International Ltd., where he was responsible for the company's CDN $70 million business unit. He was also responsible for bringing COM DEV to China and establishing its first facility in Xian, China, as a joint venture with the space research institute of the Chinese government.

Robert earned his bachelor's degree in electrical engineering from McMaster University in Hamilton, Ontario, Canada and his master's degree in electrical engineering from the University of Waterloo, Ontario. He also earned his MBA with a gold medal from Wilfrid Laurier University in Waterloo, Ontario.

Fifteen Points for Entrepreneurs

Roger Skubowius

I started Reqwireless in 2001 for several reasons:
- I thought my prior employer had great technology but suffered from bad timing and ineffective management.
- I thought the tech bubble bust in 2001 would be useful in ultimately selling Reqwireless when the bubble reinflated, as we expected to be leaders in the mobile space.
- The job situation in Waterloo was dire at that time.
- I wanted to make retirement-grade money.

From a very young age, I felt a drive to start my own company and, besides my failed enterprise at selling spider plants at the local market, it was to be my first venture as an entrepreneur. I struggled with the usual start-up challenges and dealt with the nay-sayers who said it was bound to fail, but looking back to 2001, I am certainly glad I finally acknowledged this drive and started Reqwireless. I hope you share that drive and consider listening to that inner voice pointing you in that direction.

1. Are you really an entrepreneur?

You pull into a busy mall and need to park the car. Do you cruise the outer-most spots first and take any spot and thank your lucky stars that you now can look forward to walking the near-maximum distance to the front door when there's a small chance that there's a spot right in front that you could have taken? I drive right to the front door and start spiralling out from there to minimize my distance to the door. I do this as I believe the risk is worth the reward. I believe most everyone else takes the former approach. What does this have to do with deciding whether/not to be an entrepreneur? It has to do with your innate characteristics to be one of the few leaders or one of the many followers -- to take on a high degree of risk to achieve a high degree of reward is something entrepreneurs do. Entrepreneurs are leaders of the highest degree, typically risking their finances, reputations, time with their friends and family – everything – with the hope that they'll beat the odds and score the parking spot right by the front door.

2. What to do, what to do...

When I see a problem in my everyday life, I think about what technology could do to solve it. Little self-guided cleaning robots guiding themselves through my clogged eavesthroughs is a great solution, though I settle on installing guards on the downspouts instead as no one, not even Canadian Tire, seems to sell my little robot friends. If you simply notice the impediments to what you want to achieve in your everyday life, and then consider what could be done about it to solve those problems, you'll likely stumble across a great and feasible idea in no time. In the case of Reqwireless, I simply wanted real HTML web sites on my phone, not WAP (wireless application protocol) sites that my operator charged me for.

Following this approach, I do believe there are many million-dollar ideas out there waiting to be implemented, fewer hundred-million dollar ideas and fewer still billion-dollar ideas. I also believe that most people would enjoy being millionaires, so consider focusing on an idea that solves a small problem well, instead of frustrating yourself questing for the next billion dollar invention.

3. Timing

I believe that ideas have a lifecycle – they are born, are feasible for some window of opportunity, then die. If a product failed in the past and you believe it was simply due to it being born too early for the market at that time, perhaps the market now is more receptive to it. I believe time is to a technology company's success as location is to a restaurant's success: release a product too early or late and it will fail. In the case of Reqwireless, we developed our mobile products using Java for cellphones at a time when no cellphones ran Java, but we saw the benefits of Java over competing platforms and we believed that when we came to market that Java would quickly become the standard for applications on cellphones. Java now runs on 90+% of all cellphones sold worldwide.

4. Hire great people

Your team is absolutely your greatest asset and will largely determine if your company is successful or not. As such, you need to be thorough throughout the hiring process and only hire the truly exceptional people. Do not be in a rush to bring people into your company simply for the sake of growth, take your time and hire only the very best and brightest.

I believe a few great software engineers readily beats a lot of mediocre developers, no contest. Ensure you spend the time and effort to find and lure those individuals to your company by recognizing what engineers

find important, including:
- working as part of a great team
- working on challenging problems
- getting the software they develop into production
- finding financial security inside your company

Notice "making lots of money" is not one of the elements engineers typically deem important. In my experience, quality engineers are simply more interested in solving interesting problems than discussing stock options and vesting schedules. However, that said, I also have found engineers want to know that the company is capable of paying them and offering them some upside if the company is successful.

5. Validate your idea

Make sure any idea you have solves a definable problem that exists today. As well, ensure your idea has a few revenue model opportunities to make money from. Too often I've seen technology companies start where the founders are building something that, albeit cool and fun, but solves nothing or does so for a problem that doesn't need solving. Furthermore, even if an idea solves a problem, it must have some way of making money for you. Attack your idea from the standpoints of feasibility, competition, timing – challenge it on all fronts – and satisfy yourself that it is sound. Be sure to not defend a bad idea just because it was your idea – bad ideas will fail; best to catch that at this early stage rather than after a few years of struggling with it.

6. Elevator Speech

Can you articulate your product in a single sentence so that your 80-year-old grandmother can understand what problem your product solves? Consider that your criterion when determining what idea to pursue and what product to build.

I've gone to many technology tradeshows where booths are packed with complex explanations of what the company has built and, in a lot of cases, I have no idea what they've built or what problem they're solving and I rarely see them the following year. Technologists seem to love to build overly complex products that are difficult to explain to potential customers and this can be an impediment to revenue. I prefer to build focused products that solve a very simple and easily articulated problem: Reqwireless allows users to surf real HTML web sites on their cellphones. Simple.

7. Revenue models

I think any company should have multiple ways of making money. Simply put, I think it's prudent to hedge against failure as a result of only having a single source of revenue. As such, consider multiple ways of making money from any idea you may have. In the case of internet products, think about an ad-sponsored version and a for-pay, no-ad version. Consider a consumer AND corporate version of your product as these are very different markets to serve and your product may have an opportunity in both domains. I would also suggest against any advertising-only revenue model as I don't believe advertising dollars alone can sustain most company's financial requirements except the most popular web sites and internet products.

8. Business plans

Even if you're financing the company on your own, write a business plan that minimally answers the following questions:
- What's the problem you're solving?
- What's the competition today and tomorrow?
- What are the multiple ways you're going to make money?
- What's the budget for the next year?
- What's the exit strategy?

Business plans help focus your idea and finances and, should you need to raise some money, are necessary documents for any serious investor. Furthermore, once your business is underway, you may find yourself confronted with opportunities that you didn't anticipate; the business plan can help you decide if these opportunities are consistent with your company's focus.

9. Conserve cash

Any new venture typically has the following traits:
- little money
- low company valuation (as you're just getting started)
- lots of available stock options

As such, try and weight your compensation accordingly: compensate with the least money and most stock an employee can afford to take. Stock is the motivational instrument to get long hours and good work from your team – work that will ultimately benefit you. By being generous with your stock options, you are now sharing the risk and reward with your team. Consider taking this approach with your suppliers as well – offer payment for services in as much stock and little cash as they can afford.

10. Strong drive to profitability

"Making money" was my key criterion when making decisions about most aspects of Reqwireless. If we were brainstorming a new feature, interviewing a new hire, or considering updating computers – whatever the issue– my decision-making would simply evaluate whether or not proceeding one way would likely make the company more money than not proceeding with it. Making money has the capacity to clarify the decision-making process and, especially in a small company that is struggling towards profitability, it is an essential component that should always be at the forefront of your decision making process.

11. Be fair and honest

Resist the temptation to take advantage of your role at the company and put yourself in a better position over your coworkers. As mentioned earlier, your team is paramount to your success, so ensure they participate in it should it happen. Nothing makes me happier than knowing I created a lot of wealth for a lot of employees and investors and that I started the company that brought Google to Canada and that I did it without lying, deceit or short-changing people even though doing so would have put more money in my pocket. When you ask your team to join a risky start-up, ensure they benefit from any reward that may come from it. Resist the urge to short-change them at the eleventh hour.

12. This is not a democracy

Not a lot of boats have multiple captains, not a lot of countries have multiple presidents, so ensure your company has a single leader making the final decisions and leading the company. Although your team is critical in providing input into the decision making process, at the end of the day, you are the leader of the company and are ultimately responsible for its success, so be prepared to make the decision and be prepared to rationalize why you made the decision you made. A company is not a democracy; it has to have one leader.

13. NIH (not invented here)

Software engineers seem to believe that for any code to work, they need to have written it. This "Not Invented Here" mindset can delay your product and, ultimately, cause your company to fail as your window of opportunity may close while you're spending time solving problems that have already been solved with opensource or off-the-shelf software. Creating all your technology in-house is error-prone and expensive. Use third party software to improve time to market and to keep your costs minimized. Your company needs to solve a problem that hasn't been adequately solved yet, not one that's already been solved whose solution may be available and even free to use.

14. Shutup and Listen

As an entrepreneur, you need to make a lot of decisions with incomplete information. Given your revenue comes from your customers (or would-be customers), listen to their comments and look for patterns in what they're saying to you. For example, if you're consistently hearing that your would-be customers are not buying because your product lacks a feature, consider putting that feature on the product roadmap. This may sound simple, but I've seen many would-be entrepreneurs try and dictate a product to a marketplace instead of listening to the concerns of that same marketplace.

Give your customers a number of ways to communicate their issues to you – email, phone, forum, more. There is nothing more frustrating to a user than having an issue with your product and no way to communicate that issue to you.

A direct result of listening to your customers and hearing their concerns is that your product roadmap will begin to take shape based on this feedback.

15. Monthly checkup

Try to budget time each month to step back from the day-to-day business and take a quantitative review of the key aspects of the company. Consider tracking the following key metrics of your business:
- monthly sales of each of your products
- monthly expenses per product
- website traffic and analytics
- technical support calls and emails per day and per product
- product roadmap on schedule?
- product wish list from customers on the roadmap?
- competitive landscape review
- per-product review against any agreed-upon success/failure metrics

These metrics become the inputs into a purposeful analysis of both the products and the business as a whole and will be the foundation of well-informed decision-making moving forward.

Summary

Starting a company is not for most people – there are a hundred reasons not to do it and only a few actually succeed. Before considering starting a company, be confident you possess the ability to risk it all and the focus and longevity to plan, execute, iterate and, hopefully, succeed. My top fifteen items come from my experience with Reqwireless. Feel free to take what works for you and leave the rest.

Roger Skubowius

Roger Skubowius started Reqwireless in 2001 and sold it to Google in 2005. Prior to Reqwireless, Roger worked at several technology companies in Waterloo, Japan and California.

Roger has Bachelor and Master of Mathematics degrees from the University of Waterloo. Roger left Google at 40 and spent several years enjoying time with his wife, Martha, his son Graeme, his dog Esther, his 1966 VW bus and his cottage. In late 2010, Roger launched PicoWireless, another technology company focused on mobile applications.

Ten Keys To Business Success

Jim Estill

Aristotle said, "We are the products of what we repeatedly do". Habits are the very keys to success.

You choose your habits. We are all going to have habits so we might as well make them good ones. It is easier to substitute a habit than to stop one. The best way to stop a habit is to replace it with a better or healthier habit. It is never too late to change.

1) Prioritize. Priorities change, and different situations require different skills. What might be a top priority today might be a low priority tomorrow and vice versa. The key with priorities is to think about what the important things are. It seems like shorter deadline things tend to take priority but when you look at truly successful people, they tend to focus on the long term, keeping priorities straight, and working on long term priorities and that tends to be where success is had.

2) Have clear goals. Be specific. Write down goals that are specific, measurable and positive. When you know where you want to go and what your goals are, the more likely you are to get there. Have a vision. Everything happens first in the mind. Write goals down. By writing down your goals you are showing personal commitment and declaring your intention to succeed, as well as helping to clarify your thinking. Take action. Actually take the first step you identified when you formed your plan of action. Have a time limit. Set a date by which you will have achieved each of your goals. Consider options and obstacles. How many ways can you think of to achieve your goal? Evaluate the results and consequences of each. What could stop you or cause a problem? And what about subconscious obstacles? Remind yourself of your goals, and grade yourself on your progress.

3) Nurture a network. I am constantly adding to my address book, reviewing it, keeping in touch with people and trying to add value to them. The more I nurture this network, the more I get things done. By staying in touch with friends (and most of them are friends even though I know them most through business), I tend to get more business opportunities. Sites like LinkedIn, Twitter and blogs can help you to keep in touch.

4) Be a constant learner. Change and evolve as required. This means attending seminars, reading, and listening to audio books. By making learning a habit, this could be one of your competitive advantages. It is the adaptive who thrive.

5) Be a time management fanatic. We all have the same amount of time; it is a matter of how we use it and how much we get done. Know what you have to do. I am not referring to goals here; I am referring to specific tasks. Every course and book on time management talks about the "TO DO" list or some variation on it. Part of the reason for this list is to be able to prioritize (see 1). It also helps you to know your loading. One trick with a "to do" list is to put the first action to take to start on that item right on the list.

6) Be growth-oriented. Fail often, fail fast, fail cheap. In order to move forward, sometimes we have to fail. Don't let failure stand in the way of trying to move forward. You are not a failure if you fail; you are a failure if you don't try. Growth motivates.

7) Set a pace that you can maintain forever. Although I am a big believer in the sense of urgency winning – do it now; have a propensity for action; make decisions quickly. I have found in business that the successful people are those who have a huge sense of urgency. They always want to get it done sooner and cultivate the habit of doing it *now*.

8) Welcome and embrace change. It is not only the strong who survive; it is the adapters who win. Change is opportunity. Create change.

9) Find discipline/habits. Self discipline is a key to success. Create an environment that does not tempt you not to be self-disciplined. I have more self-discipline when I take time to plan. Increase the pain of not doing something. Do not allow yourself to do what you find pleasurable until you complete the tough job. I talk to myself as a way to motivate. One phrase I repeat is "Successful people do tough things". Just saying it can be a motivator. Get support on your goals. Friends can be a great source of motivation. I have accomplished many things by just making it public that I was going to do them. Self-discipline can be learned. You can choose to be self-disciplined. It is not easy but it is what will make you a success.

10) There isn't any secret. It's all the little things.

Think about and decide what your success habits will be. Make the rest of your life begin today.

Jim Estill

Jim Estill started a technology distribution company from the trunk of his car while in 4th year Systems Design Engineering. He grew that business to $350,000,000 in sales prior to selling it to SYNNEX. He was then CEO of SYNNEX Canada for 5 years, growing sales from $800,000,000 to $2 Billion. Through his involvement in the technology space, he became familiar with many early stage companies and invested and advised many of them. He sat on the board of RIM for 13 years from prior to the company going public to afterward.

He now lives in New York and runs Canrock Ventures, an early stage technology venture fund.

Step, Step, Wow: My Philosophy on Business and Entrepreneurship

Dan Latendre

When you think about entrepreneurship, the tendency is to focus only on the next big idea. After all, entrepreneurship starts with a dream and the seed for most successful business ideas typically comes in a moment of inspiration. But while having big dreams is important, in my experience, starting small and focusing on execution is what sets a business on the path to success. Here is my perspective on the three most important considerations for scaling from the big idea to big business.

Step #1: Never Lose Focus on the Big Idea

Entrepreneurs, by their nature, are dreamers. That's perhaps the most exhilarating part of being an entrepreneur. While most people push their dreams aside and follow the crowd, entrepreneurs try to turn them into reality. We are persistent risk takers who are not afraid to fail. Willing challengers of the status quo because we know things can and will be done differently in the future.

Creating and building things is my passion. I grew up living in the country just outside of Orangeville, Ontario. My family was definitely not what you would call well-off – money was always very tight. I learned at a very early age the value of a dollar and the simple fact that you could earn a lot more working for yourself than for somebody else. Ever since I was a child, I had some form of small business in the works: selling dew worms to fisherman, cutting grass for neighbors and even writing software programs for local businesses. To put myself through university, I turned to entrepreneurship again and helped launch a successful student painting franchise that eventually grew to 26 franchisees in just three years.

After graduating from university, I had an insatiable appetite to continue building businesses from scratch and an interest in emerging technologies, so I joined an 8-person company called MKS. There I secured a grant with the Canadian Advanced Technology Alliance (CATA) and forged a partnership with Research In Motion (RIM) to launch the first wireless Internet access package, which was later bought by OpenText Corporation in 1994. Throughout my career, I've always been involved in new ventures. And IGLOO Software is particularly exciting because it's at the heart of a perfect storm in the technology sector that's bringing us closer to the concept of a virtual workplace – ubiquitous broadband access, proliferation of tablets and other mobile devices, the advent of Web 2.0 technology and the emergence of cloud computing.

Although I studied human kinetics in university, entrepreneurship has always been in my DNA. The ability to identify market opportunities, to see the convergence of external forces that enables something that was not possible before. Whether it's providing dew worms to weekend fisherman along the gateway to cottage country or identifying a fundamental shift in how we communicate, I am, and continue to be, a dreamer, a builder and an innovator. That's why you will never find me working at any large company. For me, it's simply a mismatch of culture and expectations. It's like oil and water. Entrepreneurs are not inspired by improving the corporate bottom line or driving up a company's share price. These are just outcomes, not innovation. That's why I love the Web 2.0 movement. It's driving a new era of entrepreneurship where even employees trapped in lower levels in the corporate hierarchy are empowered to make decisions. Finally, an organization's most important asset is treated as such. After all, companies don't build products, close deals or make service calls, people do.

Step #2: Start Small and Surround Yourself with the Right People

While having big dreams is important, without action, they are just that – dreams. I recommend to always start with a plan. It's almost impossible to succeed if you haven't built a roadmap. Forget the shortcuts, they almost never work. If you know the path to success is going from A to B to C, don't try and jump from A to C. Focus on executing your plan, deviating off course only when business or market conditions dictate.

When you come out of the gate, you'll want to get to a stage where you're delivering a small portion of your vision really well, to a very specific niche, market or industry vertical. Take one bite at a time and break down your dream into manageable steps that will start turning your vision into reality. Make sure you know where you want to go, but don't wait until it's perfect and don't try to build or do everything at once. Step, step, wow.

For example, at IGLOO, we operate on a very aggressive 60-day product release cycle. Sounds difficult, doesn't it? Not really. We built this into our strategy and corporate DNA. Agility and flexibility are the two most powerful competitive weapons any entrepreneur has in his tool bag. And they have been instrumental in helping IGLOO succeed in an emerging, yet highly competitive, market. We've been able to quickly respond and react to rapidly changing market conditions – both to competitive threats and new business opportunities. It has also helped us to minimize our corporate risk by delivering smaller, more manageable and higher quality product releases to our customers.

In the early stages of any company, the team, talent and expertise that you surround yourself with is critical. Start small with a very lean operation and pay particular attention to the culture. Every hiring decision matters, so make sure you bring on the right people who fit the type of culture you're trying to create. With IGLOO, I'm always looking for people with a scrappy, roll up their sleeves, "can-do" attitude. People who are willing to work hard, generate ideas and provide solutions that move the business forward.

Consider mentors. As a lean operation, it will be very difficult to maintain all of the skill sets that you'll need in-house, so the right connections and networks will be of paramount importance. After all, even the most skilled entrepreneurs can benefit from the wisdom, know-how and experience of business leaders who have "been there and done that". I've been fortunate to count two of the biggest technology leaders in the Waterloo Region as mentors: Jim Balsillie, co-CEO of Research In Motion, and Tom Jenkins, Executive Chairman and Chief Strategy Officer of OpenText Corporation. Both are superstars in their own right and each has helped to shape my approach to business, management and entrepreneurship.

Treat your financiers as advisors. Finding the right financial partner goes beyond the dollars and cents. The right partner can facilitate introductions, help open markets and provide on-going counsel and advice. That type of contribution is immeasurable.

It's also beneficial to locate your business in a region that is supportive of entrepreneurial activity. The Waterloo Region is a great example. It's a very close knit community that does a great job of nurturing technology start-ups. You've got a pool of highly skilled talent continually pouring out of three major post-secondary institutions (University of Waterloo, Wilfrid Laurier University and Conestoga College); one of the strongest support networks of economic development organizations (Chamber of Commerce, Communitech, Canada's Technology Triangle), think tanks (CIGI, Perimeter Institute) and incubators (Accelerator Centre); and all layers of government working collaboratively for what's best for the region.

Step #3: Move Fast and, When Ready, Seize the Moment

As entrepreneurs, success often depends on our ability to recognize and capitalize on change when it happens. We all know that over the past 20 years, the Internet has changed our lives forever both from a business and personal perspective. It has changed the way we work and the way we live. It has dramatically accelerated the pace of change, creating new and unique opportunities for entrepreneurs on a global scale. To give you a little perspective on the pace of change, it's hard to believe that no one had ever heard of Facebook in 2005, except for a few college students studying at Harvard. In just five short years, Facebook has grown to over 600 million members and has a bestselling movie chronicling their rise to fame called the "The Social Network". As a point of comparison, it took radio 38 years and TV 13 years to reach 50 million users.

It's no secret that the Internet and social tools, such as Twitter, LinkedIn and Facebook, are now the norm. As an entrepreneur, how you use and embrace these new online social tools can be the difference between success and failure. They help us stay connected, not only to people, but to information, knowledge and emerging trends that are happening around the globe.

Being connected is a huge competitive advantage, especially for those who know how to use these new and emerging online tools. The social movement is also changing business models, both from an operational and cultural perspective. Almost every big business now wants the soul of a start-up: lean, agile, innovative and moving at breakneck speed. Tweet, tweet.

A lean approach to business means both your successes and your failures come faster, making it far easier to quickly learn and adapt from your mistakes. Information flows are condensed making it easier to launch a project, obtain feedback and roll user input into subsequent designs and releases. You can even fail and break a few things along the way. In the end, it's like running a marathon, comprised of a series of sprints. Veering off in the wrong direction is okay because it's easy to identify, correct and get back on course.

In *The Art of War*, the great Chinese military strategist Sun Tzu references the importance of speed:

"The value of time, that is of being a little ahead of your opponent, often provides greater advantage than superior numbers or greater resources...The essential factor of military success is speed, that is taking advantage of others' unpreparedness or lack of foresight, their failure to catch up, going by routes they do not expect, attacking where they are not on guard. This you cannot accomplish with hesitation."

I have learned from experience that as companies grow larger and go public, they undergo significant changes. With scale comes a corresponding decrease in the speed at which decisions are made. Hierarchy, the fundamental structure for organizing activities in a company, actually becomes an impediment to success and market opportunities go unnoticed. On the other hand, organizations that start small and maintain a lean framework find it easier to strike fast when the timing is right. They're nimble enough to take advantage of an opportunity when it presents itself.

That's our strategy at IGLOO as we grow our presence in the enterprise social software space. Competition is fierce with industry giants like IBM, Microsoft, SAP, CISCO and Oracle vying for a share of the pie. In any market where there are established competitors, it can be intimidating, but you must find ways to level the playing field. Speed, agility and execution are my competitive weapons. While the large established vendors plan, plan and plan some more, IGLOO is executing, adapting and responding to rapidly changing market conditions. As Sun Tzu states in describing the most effective strategies, "the best policy is to attack while the enemy is still planning." Our success revolves around our capacity to innovate, self-correct and execute quickly.

It's a common refrain, but the most successful entrepreneurs dream big, start small and grow fast. And our market is no exception. In other words: step, step, wow.

Dan Latendre

Dan Latendre is CEO of IGLOO Software and a technology innovator. For more than 20 years, he has worked with such pioneering Canadian companies as MKS, Delrina and Open Text Corporation, playing significant roles in the development and marketing of numerous leading edge Internet-based technologies and applications. He has played a hands-on role in the development of the first wireless Internet access package, spearheaded the release of the first commercial search engine and helped launch the first intranet application in 1996. In 2005, in collaboration with the Centre for International Governance Innovation (CIGI), he created the first online network to help those working, studying and advising on global issues. The technology behind this network formed the basis for IGLOO Software's enterprise social software suite.

Random Nuggets:
Trust and Adaptation

Steven McCartney

Having received the rather flattering invitation to contribute to this collection I spent some time deliberating on what I might write about. With little confidence that I had something new and interesting to add to the business lexicon, I decided to contribute some nuggets offered to me by others over the years. So, if you've the patience, I am about to ramble through some simplistic learnings of mine, which as it turned out, might be simplistic but have held lasting meaning for me.

"Steven, never is a very strong word"

As a young and ambitious manager in a large corporation I was tasked with analyzing the performance and efficiency of one of our field service groups. The resulting monthly reports were shared amongst our team, a small group of line managers reporting to one section manager. At one of our meetings I got into a bit of a spat with one of my peers who took exception to the information in my report. Amongst my comments was that he never completed any of his monthly staff reports on time. Our next monthly meeting was held off-site and I drove over together with another of my peers. When we pulled up to our destination I stopped in front of the entrance to let him out before I went to park. He didn't get out right away but sat there quietly looking out the windshield. I said, "So, are you getting out?" He said, "Steven, at the last meeting when you were scolding one of the other managers for not preparing some information you said that he had *never* done it. Steven - *never* is a very strong word". He asked if it was true that our peer had NEVER completed his staff reports on time. I acknowledged that perhaps he had done them on time once or twice - but rarely. He said, "Rarely and never are not the same". Ever since, whenever I hear myself saying always, most, least, worst or never, I stop. Am I trying to over-emphasize my own opinion or am I trying to assist in resolving a situation?

For the love of a chair

Several years ago I was involved in a start-up that successfully raised sixty million dollars. I was popular, very popular. I received countless invitations; golf, lunch, dinner and coffee. There was no end of "hey, how the heck are you" at events around town. After I moved on from the firm and no longer represented significant purchasing power, my invitations dwindled down to real friends and valued colleagues and it dwindled down pretty fast. There were a lot of people who liked my chair, as did I (a very nice Herman Miller Aeron), or more accurately they liked whoever sat in my old chair. Beware the misguided ego.

Cruel but not lonely

My first real business mentor once told me, "The life of an owner-operator is a cruel and lonely existence". When the stresses increased to almost intolerable levels to whom could one turn? To whom could one talk about it? Family? Banker? Employees? No, no, and no. The solution for me as it turned out was a group of my peers. In 1995 a group of company owner-operators took the time to write a code of behaviour and to schedule monthly meetings, early breakfast, during which we would share ideas, worries, concerns and information. The most important understanding was that anything said in these meetings was never repeated outside the group – ever (Vegas rules). We slowly developed into good friends and confidants and I can assure you, the support and understanding was invaluable. I have sought out such a group twice more in my career and have always been very glad that I did. The entrepreneurial existence might still be cruel from time to time, but it needn't be so lonely.

You've just set your new price

A former customer of mine owned a small landscaping business in Central Ontario with four employees including the owner, whom we will call Don (not his real name). Don had a degree in botany and was also a stonemason. On a day when one of his staff called in sick, he decided he had better go and cut a couple of the larger lawns which his employee would normally be doing that day. One of the yards belonged to a client who had previously hired him to assist with the selection and positioning of plants to be used around the grounds of their substantial home. They had also hired Don to install a stone wall along one side of the driveway near the house.

Lawn cut, Don drove the lawn tractor up to his truck where he found the owner of the house waiting for him. After pleasantries, the home-owner asked Don what he paid his company for the grass maintenance. Don replied that they paid $50 per cut. The homeowner smiled and said, "Well, that took you a little less than 60 minutes, which means your labour rate must be close to $30 per hour. That being the case, why on earth did we pay you $120 per hour to do the plant recommendations and the stone work when you're clearly available for $30?" What value your time?

Rule number one

When you have a terrific idea, a personal ideal, or a business vision and someone, anyone, ridicules or calls your judgment into question please remember this, "If an idiot thinks you're idiot, you're OK!" This is McCartney Rule #1 – it helps prevent undue doubts and needless negative introspection. *(Feel free to pass this advice on to any young teen-ager you may know.)*

Pay yourself first

- My original thinking in year number one of business number one, "no salary for the owner, the business can't afford that yet."
- So, day of sale of business number one, I got: not a plugged nickel in value received for the work done by the owner in year number one.
- My current thinking: always pay yourself first! This even if it requires making a loan right back to the business.

Adapt to your audience

It's my second year of university and I work Tuesdays and Saturdays for Bell Canada. My job is to return to homes where a higher priced technician has installed one of a potential five jacks and complete the installation. On this day, a Tuesday, I am sent to an address just off Avenue Road in downtown Toronto. The house has been split into three units, a photographer's studio on the ground floor and two residences on the second and third floors. My customer's home was on the third floor. As it turns out, the third floor resident is a model and is working with the photographer on the first floor. Agreeing to take a break and show me where she wants the additional phone jacks, we head upstairs. She's in a hurry and walks rapidly from room to room pointing out her desired locations. She tells me she is going to take a shower and I head into the first of the rooms to begin work.

About 20 minutes later I am ready to install the last of the jacks but I can't remember where she'd asked that I put it. I knock on the bathroom door and tell her my situation through the door. She opens the door and, without her blouse, walks to the front room and points to the location again. She then promptly heads back into the washroom.

I stand in the front room flushed and a little short of breath for a few minutes. I knock on the bathroom door once again. I sheepishly tell her I still didn't know where she wanted the jack and asked if she would tell me again. She emerged, blouse on this time, and showed me once again. I installed the jack as quickly as I could and got my deflated male ego out of there. With an experienced photographer the blouse is optional; with a moronic 20-year male, the blouse is mandatory. Adapt to your audience!

A simple trust equation

In my early twenties I found myself badly wounded and disheartened by what I took as a "stab in the back" by a trusted colleague at work. My dander up, I vowed and was determined that this would not happen to me again. People would have to earn my trust before I allowed them access to my inner thoughts and ideas.

My grandfather was a true "people-person", a man with a remarkable number of friends. There was not even one occasion when was I out with him that we didn't run into someone he knew – someone who would call out to ensure a quick hello.

So it was that I asked him how he kept such a positive view of people after all this time, how was it that he had so many people he called friends. Here's his theory, only slightly paraphrased: "I could trust no-one until they had clearly demonstrated that they were worthy of my trust. Given that, I imagine I would rarely if ever be taken advantage of but I would probably only have 5 or 6 friends today. Or, I could trust and like everyone until they actually gave me a good reason not to. With this attitude, I could very well get kicked in the ass once in a while, but I might then have a thousand friends. I long ago chose the latter because I would hate to miss knowing and enjoying the friendship of the extra 995 people." Simple math.

Waterloo Region

A place where the people are almost as pleased by the success of others as they are by their own. This is a rare and powerful thing!

Steven McCartney

Steven McCartney is the President and Chief Executive Officer of Bering Media Inc., whose unique privacy platform brings real-world targeting capabilities to the online advertising industry.

Mr. McCartney was formerly a Partner of Tequity Inc., a mergers and acquisition advisory firm which provides services to North American software, hardware, telecom, internet and information technology companies.

Mr. McCartney began his career with Bell Canada, culminating a 15 year career there as General Manager Ontario, Public Communications.

Following this, he led two privately owned telecommunications services companies in the Toronto area.

From 1998 to 2002, McCartney was President and Chief Executive Officer of the first carrier in North America to provide high-speed data, telephony and cable TV services over a fibre-to-the-home network.

From 2003 until 2009, Mr. McCartney was President and Chief Executive Officer of Atria Networks LP, which owns and operates one of the largest fibre-optic networks in Ontario, where he successfully led the company through a rapid expansion including multiple acquisitions.

Mr. McCartney currently serves on the boards of Sandvine Corporation in Waterloo, Ontario and Cambridge North Dumfries Hydro in Cambridge, Ontario.

A Systems View of Business Plans

James Bowen

Too often I see business plans that are a compilation of data dumped from a web search. They have lots of data about market growth rates and about the management team but little logic and connection between the facts and figures.

Writing a business plan is a difficult job, the entrepreneurial team typically has a vision in mind that has both depth and breadth. Reducing that multidimensional image to a two dimensional paper is difficult. Sometimes ideas get lost in translation.

In addition, an entrepreneur will often get lost in data and think that a business plan full of web search results is expected. But it's not simply lots of data that makes a good plan.

Business Logic

A business plan is really about conveying the business logic behind the proposed business.

Any business is comprised of a set of pieces that have to be linked together as in a complex multidimensional puzzle. The typical pieces of business plan are management, opportunity, marketing/sales, investment, etc. Each of the pieces needs to logically connect with the others in order for the whole puzzle to hold together. It is this interconnectedness that gives the business its strength.

I will give you an example. A few years ago I was asked by a group of young entrepreneurs in Europe, who wanted to started a financial advisor service, to review their website and business model. Team members were all around 25 years of age with no experience in the industry. They were all recent university graduates. They figured their company would be the low cost competitor and would rely on word of mouth as a method of promotion, they would offer each customer a significant amount of their time to find a personal financial solution that worked for the customer. Their website boasted of their diligence and dedication with images of themselves sitting in their offices. Sounds good on paper. But we have to ask the question, what are customers looking for in a financial advisor? The cheapest costing service or the most profitable solution (for the customer)?

We can assume that most people who go to a financial advisor have a fair amount of money, in which case they are looking for a team that has dealt with similar situations to their own in the past and have come up with the most profitable solution. In fact, the cheapest service offering might attract people with smaller amounts of money so that the profit to the company from each client would be smaller than with a wealthy client. Yet each client is supposed to get lots of personalized attention. Are we looking at a low profit and low volume situation? Seems that way.

What about their advertising approach? Word of mouth. Will that work? If some of their clients have lower incomes then will word of mouth spread as quickly as with higher income clients who are more likely to know other wealthy people looking for financial advice?

While on paper the business plan seems to make sense, with a little more scrutiny it seems that the management team doesn't fit with the service offering, the marketing approach doesn't seem to fit with the revenue approach and the service doesn't seem to fit with the market. What we get from a cursory look at the example is that each piece of the puzzle has to fit with the other pieces. It is this business logic that needs to be explained in the business plan. Let us look at some of the pieces.

Management Team and Risk

Opportunities are all different. They each bring a set of assumptions and facts. Typically, any risks, uncertainties and unknowns will generate a set of assumptions. Therefore the management team will need to face an emerging or an evolving situation as assumptions are turned into facts or as the business and market evolve. In such a situation, what is the best management team? The environment that they will work in is one in which the situation changes quickly but may have indicators of change. Perhaps these indicators are based on trends or a few data points that need to be correctly correlated and interpreted. So who do we want as management? Obviously, someone who can recognize the situation that we are in and possible future states, that person needs to be able to identify courses of action to adapt the company to the most likely future states and then implement the plans. The ability to identify, develop courses of action to cover future state possibilities and then implement them that is what we want in our team. This means that someone with 20 years of experience in a large stable company or in a mature industry may not, in fact, fit the environment and could be a liability on the team.

We may also need to recognize that a high growth company could quickly go from being entrepreneurial to a more process-driven one, in which we may need the ability to replace the team and this might not match the share distribution and egos involved.

Marketing

In software there is an approach called object-oriented programming. At an abstract level, object-oriented representation categorizes the world as a set of objects. These objects have attributes and can perform functions. In marketing, we can use a similar framework to describe the capability of various marketing approaches and match them to our marketing needs. The idea is that the marketing objects that we choose should match the marketing needs object that we have.

To illustrate, assume that we have a limited market (maybe it's a niche market), limited marketing funds and a need to reach the market over a sustained period of time. These become the attributes of our marketing situation. We could also describe the market along demographic or other attributes but we are then on shaky ground. For example, perhaps we are targeting people over the age of 80 and thus conclude internet marketing is less viable. Such generalizations aren't always true.

Now we need to examine each of the marketing and sales possibilities along the same lines. Consider, newspaper advertising: it's expensive, reaches a broad audience usually within a geographical area and can be sustained over a long time period although it doesn't allow us to dynamically alter the message. But these attributes may not match our marketing needs.

Consider Twitter. Twitter can reach a carefully selected audience very quickly, for almost zero cost and can be sustained in real time as long as interesting content is available. As an example, consider the food vendor pushcarts in San Francisco, some are licensed by the city and some aren't. The police upon discovering an unlicensed vendor will fine them and maybe even impound the cart. Some of the unlicensed vendors sell homemade food items that have developed a following. Twitter has been used to broadcast to the followers when and where the vendor will be. The vendor arrives at the designated spot and time and so do the followers. Transactions are completed and both vendor and followers leave, making it difficult for the police to catch them.

Would a Facebook account work in the food cart situation? Possibly, except that the announcements are usually made shortly before the event and thus a Facebook account, not having the extreme real time attribute of Twitter, wouldn't be as effective. Consider word of mouth. It works great if your target audience knows others who are interested in the same product and willing to discuss it. As we mentioned previously, word of mouth for financial advisor services is less effective in a lower income target market since clients may have few friends seeking financial advice. Consider email: it is cheap and can reach many millions of people but has a low response rate. Perhaps that works if we don't have inventory issues or we are riding on the brand recognition factor of a well-known brand, but it's not the way to establish a brand.

What we get by considering an object-oriented perspective is the ability to consider a marketing and sales approach based on attributes such as costs, impact/results, reach, images, sustainability, etc. Such a perspective will be helpful. In business plans, we need to see a clear attribute description of both the market need and the marketing/sales approach and a logical match between them.

Financing and the Business Environment

Investment is tough to obtain and generally is seeking an acceptable trade-off between risk and potential return. Suppose our situation has many assumptions and few facts as well as a situation or business model that is sure to evolve over time. Perhaps there is an element of uncertainty in the R&D results or the movement that big players will make in their product/service offering or the evolving nature of the market. Perhaps there are competing technologies and the market hasn't decided on the winner yet. In other words, we are going to learn and adapt as we go. This situation calls for a funding approach that allows us to stay in the game for a long time, be able to fund changes in direction and not worry about irrelevant sunk costs. This implies that a financing scheme that requires short term returns and will panic over changes in direction shouldn't be considered.

Key Take-Away

The logical connection between the components of the business plan has to be demonstrated for it to be a good one. It doesn't make sense to treat each section of the plan separately as a place to dump data. Instead, we need to consider each section as an object with attributes and functions and understand how they fit with other sections of the plan including the market and opportunity. The strength of interconnectedness is what matters.

James Bowen

At age 21 and while still in undergraduate university James co-founded a software company. Over the next 20 years he and his co-founders grew an international client base. His management experience has covered all aspects of an organization including operations, business development, product development, project delivery and strategy. His technology experience included software development and consulting with a broad range of technologies. His customer experience included government, military, industry, nonprofit and educational institutions throughout North America and in some parts of the rest of the world.

Dr. Bowen has been interviewed on the internet, radio, magazine, T.V. and newspaper both in North America and Europe. He has given presentations or seminars on technology and business insights. He was the sole author of two books discussing the creation and growth of high-tech product companies. He recently published his third book "The Entrepreneurial Effect", which drew upon his wide network of entrepreneurs in a collaborative approach, focused on lessons learned from Ottawa entrepreneurs and investors.

He is associated with nine universities including three in Europe where he teaches MBAs technology, leadership, marketing, supply chain management, project management, entrepreneurship and strategy.

His volunteer work includes being a member of the Canadian Advanced Technology Alliance's (CATA) governing council and the initiator and leader of CATA's Action Committee on Entrepreneurship and his city's technology industry development agency's Innovation Leadership Team. For three years he wrote the monthly theme article discussing the technology industry and its management issues for a technology industry newspaper.

He is active with technology companies and investors and regularly provides advice to technology companies.

He is the inventor of an underwater localization system using passive sonar, a task management system and an archaeological object localization system that uses ultrasonic and infrared.

Codifying Innovation, Sharing Success

Iain Klugman

All signs point to the fact that Waterloo Region is getting it right. As a community, we're supporting tech company growth and success. And we're doing it through an ecosystem approach – all players are doing their part to make companies successful.

Historically, Waterloo Region has always reinvented itself: from buttons and rubber, to advanced manufacturing and cooperative business models, to high tech and world-leading academics. When the tech bubble burst, telecom giants fell, yet Waterloo Region remained relatively unscathed. During the recent financial crisis and the manufacturing downturn, Waterloo Region has fared well in comparison to similar Canadian communities. So what's the secret?

A large part of our success has been a highly entrepreneurial community, seized with great technology, and teeming with people passionate about living and investing here. With well over 700 tech firms, big, medium and small, and start-ups bubbling up at an unprecedented pace, we're well-positioned as a strong tech economy. It's no secret that many of our most promising start-ups have been snapped up by multinational giants like Google, Electronic Arts, Oracle and Intel. We are attracting the attention of the world: the little community that could.

But it's what fuels the entrepreneurial fire that is capturing international attention. In a place which has become synonymous with "innovation" and "resilience", the world is asking how we do it. It's one of the things Waterloo Region does better than anywhere else. The secret is in the ecosystem.

Now, put away your dusty old textbooks; this ain't your tenth grade ecosystem.

It's all about the strength of the intersections of our economy. We've achieved a high degree of collaboration among business, academia, research, government, professional services, social innovation and entrepreneurial culture. The result of this kind of collaboration is a stronger and more successful economy. You don't have to go far to find a serial CEO. Our academic institutions go beyond the theoretical and ensure our students come pre-equipped with years of work experience. Our professional firms understand what it's like to be a company whose team just grew from five to 35 overnight. Social innovators ensure we're thinking about our community and our environment when we make choices that affect us all. Our government partners understand the value of moxie, invest in us, and help us remove barriers to company growth. Our business leaders have a track record of pumping time, resources and inspiration back into the community.

As a result of a healthy ecosystem, tech doesn't just survive here; it thrives here.

Much of the work Communitech engages in goes to enabling the ecosystem. Our focus is on what strengthens us, makes us better at supporting one another, and leveraging our collective success. We deliberately focus on collaboration, creating relationships that work for mutual benefit. This focus makes us bullish, constantly seeking the leading edge of innovation, and keeping us resilient, in any economy.

We're codifying that success, capturing the model so that it can be replicated in other communities and regional innovation centres across Ontario and Canada. We're working with the new Ontario Networks of Excellence to accelerate ecosystem thinking across the province. We're coaching other regions in the delicate art of balancing sectors, nurturing all aspects of a community, and focusing on the important bits, such as attracting key talent to the region, or affecting national policy to remove barriers to foreign investment in Canada. This ecosystem approach is what drives us relentlessly forward, to discover future economic directions such as digital media, to invest in them now, to reap the benefits of foresight, and to find the courage to collectively pursue them.

Why do we do it? Because what works in the Waterloo Region ecosystem can teach other communities in Canada. And because what works in Canada's tech ecosystem is ultimately good for Waterloo Region companies.

Iain Klugman

Iain Klugman is President and CEO of Communitech

Entrepreneurship: an Eastern European Lesson

Vita Gasima

To my mind, Latvia faces the same entrepreneurial challenges that Waterloo faced forty years ago. Both are relatively smaller communities competing with larger centres nearby. Waterloo succeeded with entrepreneurial energy, dedication, teamwork and a significant measure of individual brilliance. I'd like to see Latvia become the Waterloo of the European Union. My dream is very much a work in progress, but let's take a tour of this country where I want to transplant the entrepreneurial effect of the Waterloo Region.

•

Latvia is located in Eastern Europe, and is a democratic country that gained its independence from the Soviet Union 20 years ago. 20 years' of independence experience incorporates a lot. 20 years of physical age for a person means an established personality, but on a country scale this is merely a first step. And that's where we are – finding our way in democracy by means of our own personal experiences.

During those 20 years, we've managed to establish legislation, join the European Union (EU), change the legislation again, enjoy the fastest growing GDP in EU and to experience the bite of the recession, the worst one in the respective area. Therefore everyone who is willing to start a new business in the region needs to take into consideration that we are maximalists and that a rapidly changing and unpredictable environment will require adjustments in any plans.

On the other hand – being an entrepreneur signifies exactly what is required – challenging the situation, putting together all the skills and resources, and benefiting from the circumstances. This is the task. Being an entrepreneur in Eastern Europe does not take much more than being an entrepreneur in Germany, Cambodia, India or another country – there are several requirements that apply to all countries, no matter where it is located on the map or in what stage of economic development it is.

Countless theories and books have been written on entrepreneurship and on the resources and capabilities required to be a successful entrepreneur. But let me place entrepreneurial spirit above all – identifying opportunity, setting the target – the rest is resource management in the respective environment.

We can also consider the microenvironment and macro environment challenges. Organizational – internal or micro – issues are relatively the same over the world. The most important part and the focus of this article is the macro environment, the impact on entrepreneurship from the outside – the challenge is how you will interact, particularly, with the circumstances in a particular country. So what does it take to be an entrepreneur in Eastern Europe?

Once you start thinking about doing in business there, there are several aspects that should be kept in mind.

36 Years of Independence Experienced Over a Couple of Centuries

Following the thread from present to past we must realize that Latvia as a country has 36 years of experience of independence – the number is tiny if we think and compare it with older European countries with stable economies.

Independence in Latvia was lost in 1861. After that, for more than 100 years Latvian territory was occupied by Russia and later the Soviet Union. A healthy economy is possible only in a democratic country and Latvia as a state has only 36 years of democratic tradition. As a result, the country is still at the stage of shifting values, with little stable experience to refer to both at governmental and at individual levels. The country was under Soviet governance for 70 years. In addition the Soviet era has left an indelible footprint on the mindsets of the inhabitants. It is hard for middle and older generations who grew up in the Soviet system to adapt to free market economy rules. It is simply not possible to delete all such experience from people's memories.

Market Size

As a country with its own language and culture, Latvia's market size and buying capacity is said to be lower than the average in the European Union, in terms of income and spending per capita. Because of the high level of the underground economy, Latvia's 2 300 000 inhabitants provide no reliable data on average income.

Small market size is an opportunity for small and medium-size enterprises. There is a space for players that focus on specific niches and quality. There are opportunities for local companies to penetrate the European market of 450 million people. No Latvian company so far has been successful in having a serious impact on foreign markets.

The Opportunity

The entrepreneurial effect is about making circumstances work for you, in a situation, typically, when they are against you. With respect to Latvia, an entrepreneur's perspective provides an interesting view. Located geographically with Western Europe and Scandinavia on one side, on the other side – Russia. Latvia has always interested big players as a gateway for trade and political expansion. The many types of governance that have ruled the country have left their impact on the culture and mindset. The Latvian inhabitant is flexible and open to interaction with other cultures. Small countries usually learn languages eagerly, and now the average person in Latvia knows three languages. Latvian and Russian dominate, however, English, German, French, Scandinavian are also widely spoken there. It is also easy for locals to pick up the culture of Eastern or Western businesses. The result is that a typical business opportunity in Latvia might be to become a platform for a business start-up as a gateway to both East and West.

Vita Gasima

Vita is the CEO of !MOOZ, an advertising agency in Europe and is fluent in three languages. She says, "After graduating from high school and starting to take my first jobs, I had a dream. As the final outcome of my whole working life I had a vision of a nice blue sea, Mediterranean most likely, a white sailing yacht, me with my friends on it, and bank account reports once a fortnight showing how well my company is doing received by fax machine. Since then, more than twenty years have passed and I still find myself working hard. Obviously tomorrow this vision may not be of a fax machine but Internet or e-mail and who knows what will happen during the next 20 years. And most likely my interest will be different – for now I find working life so attractive, as the knowledge and experience I gather make Monday my favourite day."

connect with the world

The legal professionals at Gowlings help bring Waterloo to the world and the world to Waterloo. Whether you are a start-up or an established tech company, we have the expertise you need, right here in Waterloo Region.

- One of the largest law firms in Canada
- 700+ legal professionals across 9 offices worldwide
- Canada's largest integrated technology law group

Contact:
David Petras at david.petras@gowlings.com or 519-575-7506
Tom Hunter at tom.hunter@gowlings.com or 519-575-7503

Gowling Lafleur Henderson LLP • Lawyers • Patent and Trade-mark Agents

montréal · ottawa · toronto · hamilton · waterloo region · calgary · vancouver · moscow · london · gowlings.c

PART II
MARKET, PRODUCT,
SALES, PEOPLE

Learning Lessons the Hard Way: The Market, Finances and People

Carol Leaman

I fell into running and advising early stage technology companies quite by accident. I was a chartered accountant, working in the corporate finance group of a local public company, mostly doing M&A and capital transactions. In mid-1998 we acquired an interest in a 20-person start-up in California called Fakespace that was struggling to find its footing. Little did I know it would lead me to what I do today and provide me with an education along the way like nothing else.

In the last twelve years I've run three start-up technology companies as CEO and have advised many others in the capacity of interim CEO/COO/CFO. It's been an exhilarating and rewarding experience learning what works and what doesn't. The biggest lessons have come from having to fix problems created by others, typically after millions of dollars had been invested and spent for little gain. That's where the story starts. There are so many tales I could recount that it would take an entire book to relate them all, so I've picked a handful that stand out. To protect the innocent, I won't mention which companies or individuals were involved in each case. In advising lots of other companies along the way, I realized that each of these stories isn't particularly unique, but I am hopeful that my experience in having dealt with them has helped others avoid many of the same issues.

The interesting grains of wisdom I'll impart involve stories related to the following:

- Understanding your financial situation and staying on top of cashflow
- Building a company while completely mis-timing the market for the product
- Not talking to customers
- People issues
- Delaying tough decisions

Cashflow

As a financial person by education, I have a better than average understanding of the importance of managing the cash resources in an early stage and/or pre-revenue company and I accept that most CEOs don't. However, it has astounded me how utterly lacking in financial competence some leaders of organizations are. The point was never highlighted to me more than in one company where in my first week on the job I discovered that the former CEO had no understanding of the difference between sales bookings, revenue recognition, collection of accounts receivable and their resulting impact on the cash forecast. But that wasn't the worst of it; in making that discovery and quickly re-casting cashflow I realized that we weren't making payroll the following week - by a lot. We employed more than 40 people, and half of them weren't getting paid. When I called the former CEO into my office (he had been moved to another role in the company by the investors) he had no explanation for it, other than to say he didn't understand it. **Lesson:** If you're running an early stage company where every penny is critical, you don't need to have an accounting designation. You need to understand basic math – as in, we are collecting $X this week in cash, and we have $Y bills to pay. Forecast that out for a year in as much granular detail as you can reasonably estimate and keep it up to date every week. You'll thank yourself. The end of that story was that I personally made up the shortfall, and was reimbursed by the investors when they could draw on their fund to pay me back.

Market Timing

Part of what makes an entrepreneur an entrepreneur is that they believe in what they're doing despite apparent odds, and persevere through challenges big or small. All too many times though, the idea that they believe in is ahead of its time, or past its prime, and they fail to recognize that and act appropriately. I've run companies that had each of these issues.

The first company acquired a significant amount of investment capital through the dot.com tech bubble and was banking on a leading edge technology that hadn't hit mainstream but that would quickly revolutionize the world – in the eyes of the former CEO. It rapidly grew to 45 people and built an expense base that was $5 million greater than the revenue it was collecting. That was fine for a year or two, because the investors funded the deficit based on the view of the CEO who "knew" that explosive revenue growth would re-set the balance and they'd be rolling in money. Except it didn't happen. The technology was way too expensive for widespread market adoption, and years later, it still is. I ended up re-organizing the company dramatically and successfully selling it to a competitor a few years later.

The second company had the opposite problem; the market existed when the company began, but the organization was too slow off the mark, built the wrong product in the wrong way and wasted a pile of time and money. Fairly early in the company's life it became apparent that the market was maturing and changing rapidly, and instead of watching the signals and adjusting, they kept hiring people, chasing the wrong sorts of customers and throwing cash at a poorly architected solution. In the meantime, competitors emerged who did a much better job of sensing market signals and built products to match. By the time I arrived at this company, the market had changed so dramatically that no amount of time or money would have made a significant difference to the outcome. I ended up selling the organization to a US software firm who ended up shutting it all down.

Lesson: Take the lean approach wherever possible and build the organization in lock-step with the market. Stay on top of market signals and when things start to change, don't hesitate to react swiftly.

Customer Discovery

Some people are shocked to learn that if you ask a potential customer what their key needs are, they might actually tell you. While the "if you build it, they will come" approach works a small percentage of the time, most of the time you'd better have a clue that someone values your idea in a way that would compel them to spend money. Really compel them. I've seen millions of dollars spent on development of "cool" products or features that no customer valued enough to write a cheque for. Talking to potential customers up front, and constantly along the way, is essential if you're going to win.

I was involved in a situation where a lot of money was spent developing a hand-held virtual reality device because it had a "wow" factor. While the development team could guess that someone might have a use for it, no one thought to actually speak to potential customers about how they would use it and what they might pay for it. Six months and hundreds of thousands later the device was finished. It *was* very cool, and we sold one of them for $5,000.

I've had to write off millions in unsold inventory, and start over from square one on product definition and development because what got built wasn't something a customer valued. Lesson? Don't be arrogant enough to think you know what a customer will pay for. If you aren't talking to them, you are almost guaranteed to make costly mistakes that sometimes you can't recover from.

People

Human resource issues run the gamut and I could write an entire chapter on the various things I've had to deal with in that regard alone. Here's a brief collection of some of the best lessons, behind each of which is a crazy story:

- a group of founders who were friends in university, started a company together, gave themselves big titles when no one knew what they were really doing, and then couldn't figure out how to have a respectful working relationship with each other. It virtually destroyed the company. Don't hire your friends unless you don't want to be friends with them anymore.
- a business founded by three brothers and their father. See above, don't hire your family.
- a senior sales guy in the mid-west whom I accidentally caught at a conference on the other side of the continent working for two other companies at the same time and in the same industry. In his four months with us he was often difficult to reach and had strange reasons for why certain accounts weren't progressing. If something doesn't smell right in terms of someone's behaviour, trust your instincts.
- an employee who tried to expense his vasectomy reversal. Pay attention to what you're approving on expense reports.
- an employee who was a performance problem who asked, in all seriousness, for a 50% raise after six months because he needed to have some cosmetic procedures done. Don't be surprised by anything.

The overall lesson: you can never predict what people will do. Just go with it, but set a tone of fair, reasonable and open in the workplace and be consistent.

Making Hard Choices

I've seen many situations in which the CEO or others in leadership positions resist making swift, tough choices to deal with issues. Whether it's an individual causing problems, or reducing costs to balance the budget, or laying people off because the business is running out of cash... it's usually difficult to get past the "hope" that somehow things will turn around and miraculously right themselves. As a result of denial and delay, critical decisions often get put off until it's too late. I've been involved in situations where problem employees that were allowed to stay drove out excellent performers, expenses that could have been cut to extend the cash runway were let go on far too long, and I've seen CEOs stay entrenched in a view about product or market viability in the face of clear evidence the company needed to change strategy. The lesson is this: if you can't see your way out of a bad situation unless a miracle happens in the next three to six months, don't wait for the miracle - deal with issues rapidly and clearly. Hope is not a strategy.

Carol Leaman

Carol Leaman is CEO of PostRank. Founded in 2007 and based in Waterloo, Ontario, PostRank monitors and collects social engagement events correlated with online content in real-time across the web. PostRank gathers where and when stories generate comments, bookmarks, tweets, and other forms of interaction from a host of social hubs. Publishers and people interested in their content use PostRank Data Services and Analytics to gauge influence and reach with audiences.

Prior to joining PostRank Carol was the CEO of RSS Solutions, the CEO of Fakespace Systems and an Executive in Residence at the Communitech Technology Association. Carol is a Chartered Accountant and sits on numerous boards of directors. She was the 2010 recipient of the Sarah Kirke Award for Canada's Leading Female Hi-Tech Entrepreneur.

How To Build a Great Product

Larry Borsato

Engineers love to solve problems.

Entrepreneurs love to solve problems *profitably*.

The difference between the two is revenue - selling the solution (your product) - to people willing to pay to solve their problems. Customers have pain, and will pay you for your product if it removes that pain. This is true regardless of what you make. People don't buy technology products because they are cool; they buy them because they are the solution to a perceived problem. (Of course the problem may just be that they want to appear cool.)

If you can solve a problem and remove a customer's pain, then you can sell the solution.

But we don't always remember that. The engineer in all of us wants to design things (software in my case) that does neat stuff. We want to build products that impress other engineers. But engineers are lousy customers. We aren't impressed by pedestrian products that just do what we need. Yet the best products are typically simple, and just work. Many companies start initially by building that flashy software, and they don't consider their path to revenue. They are in for a letdown (and often a layoff) when they realize that it isn't selling. Then comes a harsh realignment when they need to shift to mundane product features in order to close a sale. Nobody ever seems to see this coming.

This the most important lesson I've learned through years of experience building products and companies.

Build With Revenue in Mind

Make no mistake. Building software is a business. The only way to stay in business is to build a product that sells and generates revenue. If people don't value your product and won't pay for it, is there really a need for it?

I know. You have a great idea that will change the world. People will beat a path to your door just to buy it. The money will take care of itself. And that might true. But keeping the path to revenue in the back of your mind will provide the focus to make your job easier.

As you look at what to put into your product and what not to include, consider each feature based on customer value. Include the necessary and high-value features first. Add the bells and whistles later. That way you can generate revenue so that you'll have the ability to do that next release.

The first product from alchemii is *igotihav*, and it has two initial revenue streams (albeit small ones) in the first release, and a longer-term monetization strategy. These ideas were in place even before development started.

Over the years I've learned a few other lessons about building great products. I'd like to share them with you.

Build What You Know

Building a great product or service will be infinitely easier if you have experienced the problem yourself or know the problem intimately. Don't build a web-based banking service unless you know the banking business. You could hire the expertise to help but it is always better to know firsthand. If for some reason you insist on building something you aren't an expert in, plan to immerse yourself in that business.

My first company, EDRT, built student scheduling and reporting systems for Boards of Education. I was 18, had worked at a Board of Education for four years, and had just finished being a high school student. Nobody knew the requirements better than I did and that made it easy to design and build the product.

Building what you know means that you also know the pain that your customers experience, and the best way to remove it. If you can't clearly state the pain that your product takes away, then you should be concerned. The pain in our case was that school administrators had to schedule over 1000 students on paper. We removed that pain by using a Commodore PET Microcomputer to schedule them algorithmically, and then integrated the reporting system.

Build What You Believe In

Build the product that you want to with the features you believe are needed. Don't let someone talk you out of what you know, or into something you don't need either.

As you build your product (or service), you and your team (and perhaps customer) will be throwing out all kinds of ideas of what this thing can do. They all sound wonderful, and you want to implement each and every one.

For that first student reporting system, we put in everything that our premier (and only) customer asked for. It led to a perfect product for them, but a product that was virtually unusable for any other customer. As a result of that experience I learned to ask "Why do you need that?", and make them explain it to me. Once I understood I could often find another way to resolve the issue more effectively. And I learned that sometimes it is ok to just say "No".

The fact is, you will have the most passion for your product when you are building what you want to. If you believe in it, you can sell it to anyone.

Build Only What is Absolutely Necessary and Ship; Iterate Quickly

Build only the core of absolutely necessary features first and get it out in front of customers. You probably won't be able to anticipate how customers will use the product, so let them show you. Then iterate quickly in small chunks to add features that are clearly needed by the majority of customers.

Many of you will be doing a start-up as a result of consulting work, but often that work results in a product that is so customized to a particular customer that it is unusable by anyone else. *igotihav*, the product I mentioned earlier, came about as a result of consulting work with product barcodes, and a couple of unrelated ideas that I had. The first release is sparse; it does what it needs to do. The fanciest feature is its Facebook integration, but that was really a key part of the social interaction of the product.

Your product doesn't need to be a Swiss Army knife; it just needs to do a few things pretty well (unless of course you are the Swiss Army Knife company, in which case you probably don't need my advice).

But you do need to have a plan with the next steps of where your product is going. Customers - even the biggest complainers - will be much more forgiving if you are quick to fix problems and advance the product. Every customer takes a risk when they purchase your product. They've placed their trust in you. You just need to give them a little validation.

Of course that doesn't mean that you have to provide every feature that every customer wants. It's better to listen to what customers are saying and add the smaller subset of features that every customer comments on. And don't fall into the trap of copying competitors' features. Be the leader. Let them follow you.

Know Your Customer

Or more correctly, know your target customer. *igotihav* is targeted toward customers aged 18-30 who shop as well as use Facebook to interact with their friends. *igotihav* allows users to share their Wantlist - the products they want to own - with their friends, so that their friends know what to buy them for special occasions. The initial release was on

Facebook and iPhone, based on the fact that 104 million people sign in to Facebook from their iPhones every month. With only 12 million monthly users, an Android app could wait.

To meet the demands of those customers, *igotihav* needed to be able to deal with a wide variety of products from music to fashion to cosmetics. The application didn't need to be pretty, but it needed to be able to scan pretty much any product.

A different market might make different demands on your product. Knowing your customer helps you to define those needs and prioritize your development.

Don't Fear Failure

Don't be afraid of getting it wrong. *You will.* Just be willing to admit the mistake and fix it quickly. This is also why you should build small pieces and iterate quickly. It lets you fail fast and recover just as fast. You won't have that luxury as more customers come to depend on your product.

Get over your ego too. Customers have a bad habit of doing what they want with your product, even if you tell them not to. They will let you know when you screw up. Listen to them and fix the issues you hear most often.

A CEO of mine once told me "go big or go home". Back then it might have taken a million dollar infrastructure investment to deliver a product. Today I can build a product for multiple platforms with a web-based back-end, support tens of thousands of customers, and instead of begging for venture capital I can pay for it on my credit card. I can "go big" without having to "spend big".

There's never been a better time to fail. So you might as well take that risk.

So there you have it. You've got a great idea. Go for it.

One Last Thought

Like many of us, you may feel that what you created is nothing special, or something easily replicated. Get over that. You've built something incredible. Don't be afraid to tell people that.

Larry Borsato

Larry is the founder of alchemii (http://alchemii.com), a mobile social networking company, and the creator of *igotihav* (http://igotihav.com). A graduate of the University of Waterloo in Electrical Engineering, Larry has over three decades of experience as a software developer,

marketer, consultant, public speaker, and entrepreneur. He has worked with organizations ranging from one person start-ups to Fortune 500 companies with over 90,000 employees. He follows and frequently comments on technology and related subjects and loves to spot trends.

Creating Hi-Tech Success Through Market Failure

Steve Carkner

The concept of the loss-leader is not new in the retail industry. Car dealerships are particularly adept at offering cars in advertizing at incredibly low prices to bring people into the dealership, creating an opportunity to up-sell even though a few cars might end up being sold at a loss.

The concept of the loss-leader can be successfully applied by high tech companies too and can lead to great successes, if you are willing to bear the ribbing about "what were you thinking?" from a few of your investors.

The High Tech Model

We have all seen, and perhaps even been guilty of writing business plans that show an incredible adoption rate of a brand new technology. Products that will be adopted in the market and a doubling of the market that will magically take place every year for the next 5 years (or for whatever amount of time the VC's have asked you to predict in the business plan). The reality of the market is often a resistance to change and slow adoption of the new technologies. This is usually compounded by products that are close to the market requirements, but often miss a few key features that could unlock those stellar growth rates. More often than we like to admit, these first product offerings are also plagued with bugs that leave our customers waiting for revision 2.0 before they commit to larger volumes.

How can we ensure that the products and services offered to the market hit the mark the first time?

In my experience, we can't. If the product or service you are offering is truly innovative, truly disruptive, truly new… then there are simply too many risks and variables to guarantee success the first time. In fact, I would hazard that the higher the potential returns from innovation, the less likely you are to get it right the first time.

An example from the early days at RIM would be the "MPT" product. You have probably never heard of it because it was a classic loss leader, not in the sense of the cheapest jalopy on the lot, but in terms of the development dollars spent on it. The MPT or Mobile Point-of-sale Terminal was designed to bring wireless technology to credit card transactions. This was in the early 90s when the concept of wireless data, even the concept of email itself, was still very new. At the time RIM had the idea that wireless data, and building our own radio technology was a good idea, but we had no platform on which to test it.

Did we expect to sell millions of MPTs? Absolutely not. We didn't even expect to break even.

What we did expect was to develop a platform to showcase our new radio technology in a public way. From this point of view, the program was a complete success, even though total unit sales were probably only in the double digits, the device was used in public venues like baseball championships and football games, and it generated great press at the time.

Originally, when we showed the credit card companies a tiny wireless swipe terminal concept, they hated it! Their reaction was that it was too much like a toy. So we came back with a device that was big, clunky, and heavy. The credit card people loved it because it looked exactly like the big, clunky, heavy units that they were used to. Don't change too many paradigms at once!

The one paradigm we changed was the addition of wireless. The product was so big, that we were able to design the product to use an off-the-shelf state-of-the-art radio from Ericsson. Why would we put an Ericsson wireless device in a RIM product? We also built a few MPT units that had a clear back on them. These units were just as big, but they were very light, and when you flipped them over, they also had a big empty space in them… why? Because these units used a radio made by RIM. The effect was immediate with people immediately recognizing that RIM, a tiny 30 person company, had just bested world leading Ericsson. Now we had the credit card companies asking "why can't you make it smaller" and suddenly that little model we showed them in the first place made sense… the model that soon lost the credit card swipe and became a hand-held email device you see everywhere today.

My new company, Panacis, is following a similar path in the advanced power industry. We are building the worlds lightest, highest power batteries to enable new applications. But we are starting with the old applications first. One of our programs focused on retrofitting helicopters with our battery technology. Our batteries cut 2/3 of the weight off the helicopter's energy storage system. This particular helicopter is also renowned as one of the hardest vehicles in the military to start. They really have two major problems: getting it started and weight. New sensors and cargo have, over the years, pushed these helicopters beyond their original design limits, making them lethargic and prone to failure.

By performing successful engine starts on this particular helicopter and retrofitting the fleet, we will establish ourselves as capable of reducing weight on aircraft, performing high power engine starts, improving safety, fuel-efficiency, cargo capacity and reducing maintenance.

A loss leader? Absolutely. The entire fleet of this particular model of helicopter is only a few hundred, not the type of market that has the "billion-dollar" ring to it most investors want to hear. But the investment will be worth it as it opens the doors to much higher volume markets that do, credibly, have that billion dollar ring to them.

The key is to focus on the right loser (would it be too much of an oxymoron to say that I want to pick the winning losers?). You can't establish credibility by taping thousand dollar bills to every product that ships, so you need very quickly to get into the profitable sales areas. It is easy to convince yourself that every customer who walks through the door is somehow the gatekeeper to untold riches if only we could do this one little program at a loss. Soon the business is swamped with money losing programs, none of which are successful because the money runs out. Pick a few of the very best opportunities and have the will-power to say no to the rest, at least until you establish those key credibility boosting first sales that allow you to actually make money on the rest of the programs, later.

I am absolutely guilty when it comes to opening the door to too many of these programs. As the visionary in the company, it is my job to see the possibilities in everything that comes along. Ensure you back yourself up with a good team to of analyzers, financial people and program managers who have the ability to push back and help evaluate the programs. With the right balance you will pick the winning losers. With the wrong balance (too much analysis) you will end up picking no one (or they will end up not picking you because you are too expensive). With too much program management you won't take the delivery risk because everything will be padded too much, and with too much financial involvement the return on investment will never compute on programs like this because it is the intangibles that count.

How do you know when you have the right balance? Look at the team within your company that is making the go/no-go decisions on these key first programs. They are typically your executive team, often C-Level or VP level. Adjusting the balance doesn't require changing members of the team, but adjusting the dynamic. Ensure that, as the leader, you are listening to all sides equally, it may require you to be the dynamic element, pulling on your analytical side when things are getting too visionary, and vice versa. This also sets an example that your execs will quickly pick up on, you will find that, as a group, they will tend to shift and follow your lead.

Considering the decisions being made: When new customers come to you, are they thrilled that you turn around quotes really fast, yet you always lose money on the programs? This indicates that you don't have enough analysis, these are typically your operations and financial people. You may find that the marketing and engineering types are putting out proposals without even being reviewed to ensure they make basic financial sense and have at least a moderate level of planning.

When new customers come to you, are you often late getting quotes out to them, do you take far too long trying to get the legal documents just right? There is probably too much analysis involved, you may need to add a bit more risk taking to the mix. Everything you do in business will have risk, trying to minimize the risk to zero can leave a company with no customers and quickly drives the visionaries away.

The balance requirements will shift as the company matures. Early stage companies require far more vision and an ability to make quick decisions -- they need to be willing to take risks. As the company matures, more analysis is brought in to ensure that money gets made, to protect the growth that has occurred and to provide a framework and focus for the visionaries so the company moves in the right direction.

Balance the team, evaluate the possibilities and pick your winning losers.

Most of all, have fun.

Steve Carkner

Steve founded Panacis, a product development and manufacturing company in January 2002 with the goal of developing a business that would partner with customers to co-develop products in a broad spectrum of industries. This co-development model perfectly aligns the interests of Panacis and their clients to deliver strong products in a timely fashion so that all parties benefit from the market success. The business model is working well with Panacis completing three consecutive years on the Canadian Business Profit 100 list based on their 5-year revenue growth rates. Steve's strong commitment to community service and charitable work has combined seamlessly with his business goals. Several of Panacis most successful products can be traced back to charitable work done by Steve or by the company. The deep trust he inspires in both his customers, and his employees, is apparent in the loyalty that both have shown in the rapid growth of the corporation.

Prior to founding Panacis, Steve was the Director of Product Development at Research In Motion (RIM). He was instrumental in the growth of RIM from a small 12-person consulting company into a multi-billion dollar wireless-focused corporation. He is a co-inventor of the Blackberry pager and is listed as an inventor on several dozen patents world-wide. Steve also took part in the marketing and business development of the corporation playing a key role in the business development group that guided the corporation from pre-IPO in 1996 to post-IPO in 1998. Steve then became the first director of the RIM patent portfolio and led the initiative to turn the vast array of patents into an ongoing revenue stream. He challenged companies like PALM, 3COM, US Robotics, Motorola and Glenayre inside and outside of court, and won, providing tens of millions of dollars in settlement and royalty proceeds towards the ongoing growth of the corporation.

Steve has always been an entrepreneur, he started his first company at the age of 15, had four employees a year later, and bought his first investment property at the age of 17. He was a founder of Canada's National Angel Organization and was one of the youngest elected members of the Professional Engineers of Ontario council where he personally represented a ward of 40,000 engineers.

His products have won a host of awards and have been featured in places like Popular Science and the Smithsonian Institute of Technology. Steve has consistently led his teams to deliver quality, innovative products with an appropriate level of technology, market need and first mover advantage.

Market and Sell for Results

Kevin Hood

If there is one simple but extremely important message that I could provide to new entrepreneurs – it is to focus on marketing and sales from the beginning of your venture. I have seen many new ventures spend 100% of their initial time and effort focused on the creation of the product or service with little or no attention paid to an understanding of the end user. Here are "20 Questions" that you will need to answer about your business:

- What type of product/service do you sell?
- What are the major benefits to customers such as productivity improvement, better sales, profitability, expense reduction, etc. from your product/service?
- What are the comparable products/services in the market today?
- If there is nothing comparable, what are companies currently doing to perform the tasks that your product/service would do for them?
- What is the ideal type of customer for your product/service?
- What circumstances (pain/gain) should they be in to need your product/service?
- How many customers are potentially in the market for this type of product/service?
- How do you get the needed contacts or prospect list?
- Where are the best customers located?
- How many clients have used your products/services to date?
- If you have customers, how would they describe their experience with your products/services?
- What marketing collateral or tools are already in place (print, internet, etc.)?
- Has there been any publicity? If so, was it positive and helpful?
- What is the average price of your products/services and is there ongoing revenue?
- Do your products/services require specialized support and customization?
- Who do you believe would be best positioned to sell this product: you, in-house sales, external sales reps, consultants/agents, VAR's or other?
- What is the average length of your sales process?
- How many clients do you need to meet your revenue targets?

- How much will you invest in the marketing and sales efforts needed to meet your revenue targets?
- What does your marketing and sales strategy need to meet your sales objectives?

The following points will help provide a framework to help answer these questions and guide you in the development of your marketing and sales strategy.

Research

There is no better source of information about the potential of your new products and services than from the customers themselves. Endeavour to meet with, survey and speak to as many new potential end users as possible to determine if there is demand for your products and services, what their "pain" is in that area or the "gains" they are trying to make. Use this knowledge to guide your business strategy going forward. Through research we find the customers pain/gain and then we incorporate that into marketing and sales efforts. If we have identified that pain/gain correctly, we can use it in all of our marketing collateral and in direct approaches with the customers through the Value Propositions applied in our sales process. You would also need to research your competition to find out their strengths and weaknesses. Unfortunately some of these competitors may eventually copy what you are doing. Since there is no way to truly protect your IP in the long run, use the short run to establish such a strong "brand" that customers ultimately prefer to do business with you. If you ever have to fight a patent infringement in court- you will then have the revenue to do it!

Benefits/Results/ROI

Customers buy Benefits/Results/ROI–in other words, if they see no upside in using your products and/or services, chances are low that they will buy. Understanding and communicating to customer prospects the benefits of your products and/or services is a major step in ensuring long-term success. You will need to come up with the right "Value Proposition" (powerful words that move customer prospects to action). Here is an example to use: *For (target customer) who have (need/problem) the (product/ service) is a (category) that delivers (key benefit/ compelling reason to buy).*

Small Budget Marketing

Don't worry about having little or no money to spend on marketing and sales. Marketing and sales usually has to be done on a small budget in the beginning of most new business ventures. Therefore it is very important to use one of the most inexpensive forms of marketing–word of mouth. I have received some of my best business leads from people that I know who were happy to help. I once received a phone call from a friend about a project he'd undertaken. Some of the requests being made of him were beyond the scope of his expertise. In order to help his customer, he passed on my name, assuring them I had the talents and skills they needed. I contacted his customer and arranged a meeting the same week. At the meeting we talked about a number of critical issues and agreed on a strategy to meet his objectives. Within a few days I signed the biggest one-time contract of my consulting career which in turn led to several subsequent contracts and a very satisfied customer. The simple act of maintaining contact with a wide range of people is a low cost or no cost method of marketing and obtaining referrals!

The Importance of New Contacts in Marketing

New contacts are important because they increase your potential to get new information, referrals and new customers. One of the best ways to make new contacts is by becoming a member of organizations that will connect you to the right people. You will immediately gain access to a wealth of new contacts, knowledge and potential referrals. Your best new contacts are potential customers so join organizations to which they belong. For example, if you are interested in selling to local companies, start thinking about their owners and the types of organizations they might belong to. Since they are very busy, they may only belong to business type organizations such as the Chamber of Commerce.

Use Many Ways to Inform Customer Prospects

The average customer prospect may have to hear about you, read about you and/or see you many times before the circumstances are right for them to make a purchase. Here is a list of some marketing options to consider:

Association memberships

Bags/gift boxes

Brochures, catalogues

Bumper/window stickers

Business cards

Business networking

Cards/prospect

Cash register receipt ads

Charitable events

Child amusement items, toys,

Children's play areas

Clothing bearing logos

Consumer shows

Contests

Coupon mail packs

Cross promotional campaign

Customer testimonials

Demonstrations

Direct mail letters

Direction signs to stores

Discount/premium booklets

Electronic messaging signs

Email campaigns

Employee product/ service buttons

Environmental tie-ins

Event sponsorships

Faxed ad flyers

Flyers

Free information, instructions

Free trial offers

Grand openings

Greeting cards

Guest registers

Home parties

Industry directories

Internet website

Items to lend: videos, equipment

Letterhead

Logos

Magazine ads (trade/ consumer)

Mailing statement "stuffers"

Maps with ads and business location

Mascots

News releases

Newsletters

Newspaper classified ads

Newspaper columns

Newspaper display ads

Newspaper inserts

Personal selling

Personality appear- ances/endorsements

Placemat advertising

Point of purchase displays

Posters

Preferred customer events

Presentations/talks by experts

Prime business/store- front locations

Product packaging

Product samples

Public service an- nouncements

Radio advertising/pro- motion

Rebates

Referral incentives

Referrals

Search engine advertising

Seminars

Show booth/graphics

Signs for sporting events

Signs for storefront

Signs painted on vehicles

Social Networks

Special events

Specialties, premiums

Sporting event pro- grams

Sports team sponsor- ships

Store displays

Store P.A. system

Student yearbooks

Telemarketing

Television advertising/ promotions

Thank you cards

Tours of stores and factories

Trade shows

Transit ads

Two for one offers

Uniforms

Warranty cards

Window banners

Window displays

Yellow pages

Figure 1: Advertising Approaches

Are there others you can think of?

Your objective is to ensure that you use as many different types of marketing as possible to ensure that they get your marketing message.

You would should try and have 10 to 20 different marketing activities in place at all times so that your "Brand" can get established and remembered.

Selling: A Natural Extension of Good Marketing

Successful marketing predisposes a prospective customer to you and your products and/or services. Using an effective combination of marketing and sales is the key to building a solid customer base to launch and sustain your new business.

If you are like most entrepreneurs, you are uncomfortable with the idea of selling. That's because you don't realize you've been selling all your life. Trying to get your way with others (often family members!), get a job, keep a job, convince a group that your approach is the best one - all of these required you to sell yourself and your ideas. The difference in business is that you get paid for what you sell!

There are many factors that influence customers' buying decisions, but none is as important as who they are buying from. The reason for this is simple. Customers will only buy from you when they trust that you can deliver the results they want. That's why it's important to build rapport and trust as a prelude to generating sales. Trust is created from a professional and thorough approach that helps customer prospects make great buying decisions. Your attention to their needs, your ability to fix a "pain" or help them make a "gain" will create the basis for a long term customer relationship. Your goal should be to have "repeat" and "referral" customers as the vast majority of your business. The value of your business increases with the strength and retention of your customer base!

Define Your Sales Process

Every sale requires a step by step process to help the customer reach a decision. Every business has a different sales process.

The retail sales process is as follows:
<u>Retail Sales</u>

Greeting   Questions   Review Options   Decision
3 to 60+ minute sales process

Compare this to the consulting sales process:
<u>Consulting Sales</u>

Call   Contact   Meeting   Proposal   Decision
1 to 6+ month sales process

Every business is different so the objective is to define and completely understand the steps required for you to close your sales. I suggest creating a binder with tabbed sections for each step in your sales process. Create and document the information needed at each step including phone scripts, meeting agendas, needs analysis templates, sample proposals, typical objections with answers, trial closes and a good closing methodology. This will formalize your sales process, help you achieve your initial sales and eventually be a great tool for training new sales representatives.

Understanding the Prospect to Sales Ratio of 10-3-1

Every new business will go through a cycle of learning who the best customer prospects are and fine tuning the marketing and sales approach. One thing is clear though – you can do everything right but still have an unreceptive customer prospect! This is known as the 10-3-1 prospect to close ratio. For every 10 prospects you speak with, only 3 have the right combination of circumstances at that moment to want to learn more and only one of them will be able to follow through to a closed deal. That is not a bad situation to be in. You educated 10 prospects on your value proposition, got three of them to meet and one to buy. This is an on-going process with many prospects as possible at any given time so you should always be in a position of producing your next sale. The ratio can improve dramatically the longer you are in business because you start to earn more repeat and referral customers – so the ratio may change from 10-3-1 to 10-6-3 and then 10-8-6, etc.

Post Sales

This is where the real long term relationship with the customer begins. Exceed their expectations and thrill them with your attention to detail! The repeat business opportunities will be there and the word of mouth referrals will be there. Make sure that all people involved with the customer have the same customer service standards that you do. Train them and support them where needed because the long term viability of your business depends on it.

Summary

If you focus on the marketing and sales requirements for your business from the very beginning you will get an important understanding of your marketplace, the size and nature of the opportunity, the "pains" and "gains" on the minds of your customer prospects, the words you will need to use to get their attention, the trust-building focused sales process that will close the deal and finally the customer service that will secure them as a long-term customer!

Kevin Hood

Kevin Hood, founder and President of Market Access Corporation, is described as an innovative, creative and results driven entrepreneur and has over twenty-seven years' experience working with new entrepreneurs, start-ups, emerging companies and major corporations. He provides consulting, training and recruiting services to a wide range of companies. Client Companies have included IBM, CIBC, Northwestern Mutual Financial, Microsoft, Philips Electronics, Maplesoft, the Canadian Professional Sales Association and many start-ups. He originated and co-developed the "Tech Sales Program" to teach tech entrepreneurs how to achieve sales results. At the University of Waterloo Accelerator Centre, Kevin Hood provides marketing and sales mentoring services for the start-up and emerging tech companies that are resident there. He also teaches marketing economics part-time at the University of Waterloo.

Think Big! Build Your Sales and Marketing Processes Properly - Right from the Get-Go

Rick Endrulat

Introduction:

So you've got your product or service to market – congratulations! You may even have some key customers, partnerships and references. But now what? Here comes the fun part: How do you sell your product or service and continue to acquire new customers and build your customer base?

As entrepreneurs, we sometimes get very focused on building a great product or service and taking it to market. However, this is just the beginning – there is lots of hard work still required to sell and build your customer base to fuel your company's growth. And you do need to keep building your customers – this is no time to rest on your laurels.

As a fellow entrepreneur I understand the cash flow concerns in the early stages of *any* company. So, I've put together some tips and techniques that have helped my clients and me as we were growing our businesses. Find what works for you and watch your sales grow!

Challenges:

Many entrepreneurs are great engineers or technicians. However, people who are great at the technical aspect of their product or service are not always great at selling their product or service. To be good at selling, sometimes it's better not to be the technician – which means you need help! However, there are some real challenges that await the entrepreneur building a sales team:

Resources – Who will run sales? Who will run marketing? Who will manage the process? Any way you look at it, there is the need to get some help. But how do you find qualified individuals? How do you find someone you can trust to understand and help grow your business? And, of course, you need to have someone who can run the right types of sales and marketing programs that will drive real business for your organization.

Cost – Once you do find someone, can you afford them? A senior level resource can be a huge investment for an entrepreneur. And the cost of marketing campaigns can also be prohibitive – advertising, PR, direct mail, and other marketing activities can drain your cash reserves. – You need to ensure you are spending the right amount of money on activities that drive a significant return on investment.

Sales Optimization – Once you have your marketing and sales process established and you are generating leads and sales opportunities for your sales team (even if that is only you), it is important to retain the correct focus within your team. Recent research from CSO Insights shows that sales representatives only spend approximately 36% of their time "selling." The rest of their time is split between administrative and other non-revenue-generating tasks.

Solutions:

So what is an entrepreneur to do? Below are some tactics that have helped early stage companies successfully grow their business and grow their client base over the years:

Strategy 1 – Build a Structured Sales and Business Development Process from Day 1

Even though you may be in the early stages of your company, it's important to structure your organization as you need it to be years from now. Part of that is building your overall sales and business development plan from Day 1.

Market Readiness and Strategy – How is your product/service different than the others? Are you developing a new market? Creating a niche? Expanding into an existing market? These are all important questions in your early stages – and ensuring you can clearly articulate your plan and your key strategies to realize this plan is important. Many companies fail at this stage – even though they may have a very strong competitive advantage. If you need help, this is an important stage where an outside consultant or advisor could provide some additional guidance. In fact, many companies form advisory boards for this sole purpose – to get access to knowledgeable industry experts, and to 'stress test' their strategy and their go-to-market plans.

Sales Tools and Development – Once you have your strategy developed, it is important to translate that into a well-defined plan. Have you established sales goals and targets? Do you have a detailed plan to get there? Can you articulate what is in it for your customers if they use your product or service? Your sales team (whether they are internal or external to the organization) need guidance, and also need the tools to help them succeed. Developing a plan and the necessary materials your sales team needs will help ensure that they are communicating the right things to the market. Don't leave it up to chance – try to develop as much consistency as possible across all of your communication methods.

Target Market Development – Once you have your sales plan, you are ready to start communicating to your target market. Now – have you defined your target market? Can you break down which industries you are most successful in? What about the company demographics (revenue, employee size, geographical region) of your best prospects? And once you have your target companies, who do you sell to within those companies – what title? What roles/responsibilities? Developing your target market database is a key step in your process – utilizing services like Dun & Bradstreet, Hoovers, and other crowd-sourced online databases like Jigsaw will help you build some good contact lists and prospect databases. Targeted associations and other directories can also provide good sources of prospects for you. But make sure you spend the time building a good quality, targeted database – otherwise you will be wasting your time selling to the wrong people.

Demand Generation – Do you know how to effectively reach your target market? Find what works in your industry to generate new leads. Look at your target market and see how others sell to them – do they attend tradeshows? Do they attend online webcasts? Respond to direct mail? Look at where others are having success selling into your target market and try to emulate other successful strategies.

Sustain your pipeline – How do you ensure that once sales start pouring in, they don't stop? To keep a steady flow of sales, you need a steady flow of leads. And that means you need to keep the leads flowing through various marketing and sales tactics. Whatever works for your organization – keep it going! As entrepreneurs, we may focus our time on closing a large or strategic deal. However, while we are doing that, we are losing sight of prospecting and finding the **next** big client. So don't let the big fish distract you – keep your lead generation activities going steadily and you won't see a drop in sales activities.

Measure your success – How do you track your business' success? How do you track the success of your marketing and sales efforts? Ensure you have the systems in place to measure your activity. CRM systems have become much more attainable and easy to implement. Marketing automation systems can help you convert and nurture leads. Whatever you use, ensure that you have a system in place to measure your activity – and then use those metrics to improve upon your overall performance.

Strategy 2 – Let Others Sell for You

Are you feeling overwhelmed by the amount of effort required to build your sales and business development process? Unsure how you will find the time or resources to implement the plan? Well - what could be better than having someone else sell your product or service for you? Sound too good to be true? Well, I've seen it happen many times in the past.

Talk to your customers – Engage your current customers in conversation. If your clients are happy, they'll enthusiastically provide you with feedback that can help you sell: What is it about your product/service that they liked? What resonates with them? But don't stop there – ask them for a referral. Many clients are happy to tell their colleagues about vendors they are satisfied with. You'd be surprised by the great referrals your clients can provide. Once the new clients start rolling in, make sure you don't forget about those first clients that helped you build your business!

Find some partners – No, I'm not talking about financial partners, although additional cash is always welcome! Look at your product/service, map out your value chain, and see if there are complementary service providers or vendors that could provide strategic value to your organization. Perhaps it is a consulting firm that works in your space. Possibly it is a vendor you currently use or integrate into your product or service offering. Regardless, it may be worth a conversation to see if there are joint selling opportunities or ways you can leverage their customer base to sell into! And don't forget about associations and other organizations that may provide access to some targeted members for you. If you can show the value of your product/service they may work with you to help promote your company.

Be careful that you don't spend too much time working through partnership details, and not enough time building joint revenue! Finding that first joint client or sales opportunity is a great test of the partnership and indicator of the synergies within the partnership. Although defining and documenting partnership terms are important, never lose sight of the financial requirements of the partnership – I have found that focusing on some short-term sales opportunities will ensure that both parties see the financial viability of the partnership early on. This will then ensure that each partner is more committed to the continued building and growth of the partnership. Use these early clients to evaluate your partnership terms and evaluate the long-term potential of the partnership – if the terms don't make sense once they are applied to real-life clients and sales opportunities, it is time to change them! Better to make this decision early on than to suffer in a non-productive partnership.

Conclusion:

Starting a company, getting a product or service to market, and growing business can be immensely challenging. However, that is only the beginning. You still need to sell your product/service and increase your sales. By building strategic partnerships, strong systems, and effective processes, any entrepreneur can develop a consistent and repeatable sales activity flow that will help them grow their business successfully!

Rick Endrulat

President, Virtual Causeway North America. The firm's clients include leading brands such as RIM, Sybase, OpenText, HP, EMC and Oracle as well as other emerging brands. Under Rick's leadership, Virtual Causeway has grown rapidly and was recognized for three years as one of "Canada's Fastest Growing Companies" by *Profit Magazine*.

In addition, Rick is a strong supporter of non-profit organizations. He is a founding member and on the Board of Directors of Sustainable Waterloo, an environmental non-profit organization. As an advisor to Wilfrid Laurier University's Schlegel Center for Entrepreneurship, and a mentor with the Canadian Youth Business Foundation, Rick advises young business leaders and coaches them in their development. Rick has a Masters of Business Administration from Wilfrid Laurier University and is a Quantum Shift Fellow with the Richard Ivey School of Business at the University of Western Ontario. In 2009, he was recognized as one of Waterloo Region's "40 Under 40." Rick has also received Wilfrid Laurier's MBA Alumni Award in 2008, and Communitech's Tech Impact Award for outstanding leadership and involvement in the local technology community. rick@v-causeway.com, www.v-causeway.com

Managing Growth

"Companies grow like kids: every seven years or so they morph into something completely different."

Randall Litchfield

Now that our company is seven years old going on eight, it's uncanny how everything you learned as a parent about the stages of child growth comes back at you. Children grow incrementally for years then suddenly morph into a new animal approximately every seven. That's how it feels today. When we hit $3.5 million in sales last year it seemed that every system and procedure we had developed since start-up was suddenly obsolete and over-taxed.

The other parallel with child development at this stage is how the company seems to take on a mind of its own. Granted, as a digital messaging company, we are in the knowledge business and the only smart way to run a business like this is to hire people smarter than yourself. Nevertheless, entrepreneurs tend to create companies in their own image; an extension of their personalities, skill sets, values, work ethics and (mostly) egos. This works through the start-up phase, the early growth phase and even the what-initially-looks-like-maturity phase. But it inevitably hits a ceiling when, suddenly, the company no longer looks like its founders at all. It has outgrown them.

This is my world. As the CEO of a rapid-growth company (we have made Profit Magazine's 100 Fastest Growing Companies list for the second year running), I scratch my head wondering why life isn't getting easier. For all of its outward appearance of shining health, Inbox Marketer has internal growing pains that ache like appendicitis. Any business owner having passed through this growth phase will recognize the symptoms:

Breathing room - we're re-locating for the fourth time in seven years. Every time we re-locate I think we've taken care of the next five years only to be disappointed by year two. The barometer is always my own office, which begins large enough to hold sizable meetings and ends - well - I don't really have an office at the moment.

Dated processes - Those production, invoicing, timekeeping, HR and accounting processes you set up years ago when you had six people? They're not cutting it anymore now that you have 26. That well-oiled, internal efficiency you project so well to clients threatens to break down at the most damaging times.

Stumbling on first names - Granted, I'm not getting any younger and have a problem remembering names anyway, but recently I met an employee for the first time at a company gathering. This has never happened before and it is not that long ago that I hired everyone personally.

Growth ceases to be fun - Never thought I'd catch myself muttering that. But growth is only fun when everyone enjoys their work. When stress levels build because growth strains your existing processes, people and infrastructure, it's time to retool (itself a stressful exercise). And at this particular stage, it is not the normal, incremental retooling you've performed so flawlessly in the past. We're talking transformational, gut-wrenching change.

There are more symptoms but, the point is, we have *$3 million-itis*. It's when companies typically find that the systems and procedures that served so well from start-up, now strain under the accumulated weight of those years of growth. Our accountants, lawyers and other trusted business advisers say this is classic. All we have to do is a proper job of retooling and we should be good for $10 million.

So that's where we are - retooling for a $10 million Inbox Marketer. Bearing in mind that this is all very much a work in progress, here is what we have learned so far:

The first thing is to *lose the denial*. It takes a while to admit that you're stalled, especially when you continue to "grow". But this is the growth paradox - it isn't real if it isn't sustainable. If your company can become unglued in mid-flight because of dated processes you can do a lot of *ungrowing* really fast.

We're particularly sensitive to this issue at Inbox because so much of what we do involves managing enormously complex messaging campaigns for some enormous clients. When things go wrong, it's never in front of a few people, but a few million. The production processes we invented years ago when our campaign volume was a fraction of today's, still serve us. We've dodged all the bullets so far, but it only takes one or two to cut down your carefully built reputation.

The second thing is to *bring in the professionals*. Because you've been so successful, you probably have a great track record of retaining people that you groomed over the years to be your senior team. If you are in the technology business like Inbox, they may even have worked for you most or all of their careers. They perhaps - naively - consider your company to be the managerial norm rather than this idiosyncratic extension of the founders' alter egos. This is where you need good external, professional, management training. Your team needs other mentors than you, and you need new points of view. So send the people who actually manage off for formal training in how to do that.

Personally, I benefited hugely from my pre-entrepreneurial years spent at some of the world's best-run corporations, especially my first employer out of university - Procter & Gamble. Here I learned formalized management processes, forecasting, business communications (P&G's famed edict of single page memos is still the best writing lesson I have ever had) and corporate ethics. In short, I experienced first-hand a successful corporate culture and how it sustained itself. Although I still adhere to those management practices and try my best to pass them on to my team, the training environment just isn't the same - the difference between Harvard and a one-room schoolhouse.

Thirdly, *get the fundamental procedures right*. These can vary by company, I suppose, but *accounting* and some form of *production system* usually top the list. On the accounting side, I'm told our off-the-shelf accounting software is probably good for $10 million, but our own procedures are not. Here, we rely heavily on the consulting expertise of our accounting firm to help us retool and retrain.

On the production side, we are re-coding just about all of our production and messaging software. In the beginning, we purchased much of our messaging technology and focused our business around client strategy and customer service. Then we *continuously improved* by surrounding these store-bought systems with our own enhancements based on our growing expertise in our own industry. Then *we* became the leading experts and now our enhancements painfully outshine the original purchased components. Solution? Rewrite everything as an integral package that gives us a strategic, competitive advantage.

Fourth, *don't short-change HR*. You feel *$3 million-itis* most acutely in HR. It used to be your office manager's part-time job, and what filled their time between bookkeeping, ordering supplies and organizing the office Xmas party. Now it is a strategic imperative. If you're in the service business like most of Canadian GDP, your principal assets come through the front door every morning. We've put all our main HR policies under review, from compensation to employee training. The operative word is *formalization*. Our big discovery on HR policy is that, the more people you have the greater the need for articulation. Your employee growth may be arithmetic, but the opportunity to misunderstand is geometric. Our first employee handbook comes out this month.

Fifth, *hire from your best customers*. Please don't jump to the conclusion that we purposely pillage our customers for people. We don't, but somehow some very seasoned former customers have ended up working here (usually having spent an interval somewhere else).

I have to say that former customers are among our best hires. One sure reason is that they *get* the culture. In our case it is a customer service culture and the reason why these former taskmasters selected us as vendors in the first place. The second reason is that they bring a client-side perspective of our company that is difficult to get otherwise. Thirdly, they usually hail from very large companies. Not everyone can make the adjustment from a large to a small company, but the ones that can bring great insights and add significantly to your gene pool.

No one is more overwhelmed than me by our growth and success. In the beginning it was a constant effort to accelerate and drive the business. Today it seems a constant effort to keep from running off the road without actually slamming on the brakes. If you'll forgive another car analogy, sometimes we feel like the dog that caught the bumper.

Successful parenting means a gradual loss of control of your children as they grow and become their own decision-makers. That's what running a growth business means as well. Your job as parent/CEO gradually reduces – for lack of a better term – to guidance. You steer, train, reinforce company values, maintain a happy and rewarding culture and make sure the house is big enough to accommodate everyone with no line-ups for the bathroom.

Inbox resembles its parents less and less each day. All the turmoil has made one lesson abundantly clear: when *$3 million-itis* hits, the real growth strategy for entrepreneurs is planned obsolescence – your own.

Randall Litchfield

Mr. Litchfield co-founded Inbox Marketer Inc. in 2001 and is a publishing professional with 30 years experience in print, Web-based and email publishing. His career from 1974 to 1994 was that of a business editor employed by the country's largest print publisher, Rogers Publishing Inc., directing well-known titles such as Canadian Business Magazine and Profit. In 1994 he founded Demand Systems, an Internet publishing company he built over the course of six years and sold to a large US e-commerce company, VerticalNet, in 2000. Mr. Litchfield holds a Masters degree in International Relations from the University of Windsor and is a graduate of the Queens University Executive Program.

Ten Common Legal Pitfalls for Technology Entrepreneurs to Avoid

Tom Hunter

I often view an entrepreneur as an energetic, optimistic puppy dog and a lawyer who advises him as a cautious and wise old cat. How can these two opposites work together, and not against each other, to avoid the common legal pitfalls that plague entrepreneurial start-ups and early stage technology businesses? By addressing ten of the most common legal pitfalls which technology entrepreneurs need to avoid to survive, it can be demonstrated that the chances of survival and success are greatest when the technology entrepreneur and their legal counsel work together to avoid these pitfalls. Rather than putting the pitfall in the negative, the title is the solution, and an explanation follows:

Pitfall #1 Ensure That You Own Your Intellectual Property

Every entrepreneurial technology business has a great idea or two that are developed and moulded into a new product or service. The development and moulding is most often done by multiple individuals – the founding entrepreneurs themselves, students, employees, consultants and even family and friends. This development history worries legal counsel. Why? Because every contributor to the development of the ultimate product or service has a potential ownership claim which either must be waived or transferred to the entrepreneur or his or her emerging company. Entrepreneurs do not necessarily appreciate this legal pitfall, especially when they feel that an individual may not have contributed something valuable or useful to the technology development.

When this ownership issue is raised by legal counsel, the entrepreneur often just wants this ownership issue to simply "go away", as after all, the entrepreneur "knows who the real contributors of value were". Legal counsel will point out that the entrepreneur's opinion of who contributed "value" is largely irrelevant and that each contributor's potential ownership claim, valuable or not, may have legal merit. Working together the entrepreneur and their lawyer can analyze the potential claim of each contributor and agree upon an effective strategy to deal with each – some will be asked to sign a waiver to release any ownership rights, some will be asked to execute an assignment to transfer any ownership rights and some will be left alone as their rights may be negligible. This approach will ensure that an entrepreneurial technology company can represent and warrant to financiers, acquirors and other third parties that it owns the technology it has developed and which forms the basis of its innovative product or service. Should the technology company be unable to make this ownership representation and warranty, then it will be exceedingly difficult to raise money, attract talent and entertain the offers of interested acquirors.

Pitfall #2 Adopt, Implement and Massage a Patent Strategy

Entrepreneurs see excitement and opportunity behind every door. Lawyers see emotional stress and disaster. Having established the ownership of the intellectual property underlying the technology company's product or service, it is vitally important that this intellectual property be protected. Although entrepreneurs understand the need to protect their company's intellectual property, they often view this task as an overly expensive one which can either be avoided or at the very least delayed until the company achieves substantial and recurring revenue – after all, "the intellectual property underlying the product or service is obviously brilliantly innovative, is it not? Maybe we should just keep it a secret since no one else will have created anything like this?" The lawyer's view is influenced by negative and recurring thoughts of:

(a) The possible infringement of third party patents by the technology company's intellectual property;

(b) The rare existence of brilliantly innovative intellectual property/ technologies;

(c) The wasted time, effort and money that successfully attacked intellectual property means to a defendant technology company; and

(d) In the worst case scenario, the possible elimination of the entrepreneurial tech company as a going concern if it can not successfully defend itself from patent infringement claims.

Keeping intellectual property or innovative technology a secret is a naïve and imprudent business strategy. Corporate espionage, a transient work force, on-line security breaches (e.g. WikiLeaks) and the use of patent infringement lawsuits as a method of doing business have rendered this business strategy obsolete in protecting a technology company's core intellectual property. The entrepreneur and lawyer working together can build and implement a strategic and flexible patent strategy to protect a technology company's core innovations and in so doing secure competitive advantages for the company in its target market. Can you imagine being the only tech company in your target market legally entitled to offer your customers a highly valued product or service feature? Only a strategically built and managed patent portfolio protecting the company's core and blossoming innovations offers this compelling competitive advantage.

Pitfall #3 Arrive At a Marketable Product or Service

Brilliant technological inventions which are patent protected and yet "sit on the shelf" and never reach a customer are a cliché. Why is this the case? Entrepreneurs will usually take many years and spend thousands of dollars to develop and protect innovative technologies. However, do those innovative technologies address a problem which is widely prevalent in a particular market? Too many entrepreneurs see the development of an innovation or the completion of an invention as an objective in and of itself. Lawyers in this field advise entrepreneurs to focus on serious problems which a market or industry is experiencing and to use their technology development process to create an innovation which will solve or reduce the effect of that problem. If the problem is serious and widespread and the technology innovation substantially reduces the effect of the problem or provides a complete solution to same, then the innovation can form the basis of a "must have" product or service for customers in that market or industry. Lawyers can work with the entrepreneur in determining whether a problem which is perceived by the entrepreneur to be serious in a market is in fact so and also if the entrepreneur's proposed innovative solution is "open" for development by:

(a) Preparing appropriate non-disclosure agreements for use by the entrepreneur as they discuss their proposed innovative solution with parties who are active in the target market (i.e. academics, established businesses, professional service providers, consultants, financiers, regulatory bodies etc.);

(b) Completing appropriate patent searches in jurisdictions where the market problem is perceived to be prevalent in order to determine if the entrepreneur's proposed innovation is already in development by another entity. This will also assist the entrepreneur in assessing his or her potential competition; and

(c) Drafting and negotiating joint development agreements with strategic partners to increase the effectiveness of and the speed at which the entrepreneur's innovation might be developed.

A "must have" product or service which is based upon innovative and patent-protected technological inventions is unlikely to ever "sit on the shelf" gathering dust.

Pitfall #4 Develop a Working Prototype of the Product or Service

A rational financial investment atmosphere, such as the one we are currently experiencing, demands that entrepreneurs created a working prototype of their product or service in order to attract seed capital. The prototype need not be of a commercially finished nature, but it must reliably demonstrate how the new product or service solves or fundamentally reduces a serious market or industry problem. The need to develop this prototype is not likely lost on the entrepreneur, but legal counsel can recommend a number of actions to avoid those legal pitfalls which arise at this stage of the entrepreneurial development process, including the following:

(a) Require all third parties who are being interviewed to assist in the design, development and/or manufacture of the prototype to execute an appropriate non-disclosure agreement prior to material discussions being undertaken;

(b) Ensure that those chosen to assist in the development of the prototype execute formal contracts in order to ensure that all rights associated with the design, development and manufacture of the prototype become the property of the entrepreneur's company. Such contracts must be entered into before the retained party commences their work;

(c) Ensure that all third party contracts set out the material deal points pertaining to the design, development or manufacturing tasks, including third party qualifications, expertise and experience, prototype specifications, required deliverables, timing expectations, ownership rights and third party compensation details; and

(d) Ensure that the technology company "massages" its patent strategy to contemplate changes or enhancements to its current, or newly created, technological inventions which are revealed in the prototype development process.

Too many entrepreneurs skip or casually address these action items only to create, of their own doing, a wholly negative prototype development experience the legal ramifications of which may be fatal, or at the very least, damaging to the business and not easily remedied.

Pitfall #5 Demonstrate Customer Traction

An innovative and legally-protected product or service are not the primary objectives of a pragmatic entrepreneur – satisfying customer need, and achieving significant sales and profits as a result are the fundamental objectives. Nothing excites potential investors like customer traction, but one should not confuse positive reactions and feedback from potential strategic partners and customers with actual and verifiable customer traction, and unfortunately entrepreneurs often make this mistake. Legal counsel can define "customer traction" in concrete terms for the entrepreneur to pursue in the following basic forms:

(a) Customer Surveys – products or services which target consumers can be made the subject of formal and statistically sound surveys conducted by nationally or internationally recognized public opinion companies. Results of such surveys are prima facie evidence of customer interest in the proposed product or service. The purpose and scope of such a survey should be reflected in a detailed contract executed with the public opinion company;

(b) Joint Development Agreement – this type of legal contract is often utilized by the entrepreneurial company and an established company in the target market to bring the entrepreneurial company's embryonic working prototype to a commercial state. Sourcing, negotiating and executing a formal joint development agreement with an established company is substantive evidence that an experienced company in the target market is of the opinion that the product or service will attract customer interest;

(c) Field Trial – often the first opportunity for a customer to use the product or service in a commercial setting is facilitated by the conduct of a field trial by the entrepreneurial company and a strategic partner (often a company in the target market with access to customers/clients who will "trial" the product or service). Although the parameters regarding the product or service trial are tightly controlled, legitimate customer or client feedback is obtained. This feedback together with all other results of the field trial are made available to both the entrepreneurial company and the strategic partner. A positive field trial is direct evidence of customer interest in the product or service;

(d) Market Entry Agreement – a successful field trial can often lead to a joint marketing, joint distribution or licensing agreement whereby the entrepreneurial company offers its product or service to a target market by accessing the distribution network and/or customers of an established vendor in that market. Such a contractual relationship requires comprehensive negotiation, a thoroughly vetted contract and appropriate legal and tax advice since this is the first attempt to sell the product or service in the open market. This type of agreement is the next to best evidence of customer traction; and

(e) Sales – if all goes well in step (d) above, then the chances are good that there will be actual arm's length commercial sales of the product or service to customers or clients in the applicable target market. Legal counsel will work with the entrepreneur to ensure that such sales are made upon such binding terms, conditions, representations and warranties as are desired by the entrepreneur by preparing the proper legal form of sales contract (i.e. purchase order, sales contract, license agreement etc.). Obviously, multiple arm's length sales of the product or service to customers or clients is the very best evidence of customer traction.

Pitfall #6 Acknowledge The Role Of The Team

Unconstrained by traditional thoughts and practices, entrepreneurs are by nature independent self-starters who enjoy the creative process and the autonomy and responsibility that goes with starting one's own company. However, an entrepreneur's nature left unchecked can inhibit the chances of commercial success. If however, the entrepreneur can acknowledge the role of the team and delegate authority and responsibility to well-sourced and well-chosen team members then the entrepreneurial company's odds of success will skyrocket.

Legal counsel can assist the entrepreneur in defining, sourcing, retaining and managing the "team". But who precisely is the "team"? Many entrepreneurs make the mistake of thinking that the team consists only of the entrepreneur and the employees and independent contractors who are hired or retained to work for the entrepreneurial company. However, knowledgeable legal counsel will impress upon the entrepreneur that the "team" is most strategically considered to consist of all of the following parties:

(a) Founders – the entrepreneur or entrepreneurs;

(b) Shareholders – usually consisting of the founder(s) and those who invest funds into the entrepreneurial company;

(c) Board of Directors – individuals elected by the shareholders to set the strategic direction of the entrepreneurial company and who are ultimately responsible for its success or failure;

(d) Officers – individuals appointed by the board of directors to manage and be responsible for the day to day operation of the company's business, including the president, chief financial officer (CFO), chief technical officer (CTO), secretary, treasurer and vice-presidents (i.e. sales, marketing, production, development etc.);

(e) Employees – individuals hired to assist the officers in carrying on the day to day business of the entrepreneurial company;

(f) Independent Contractors – individuals (i.e. consultants) generally retained for specific company projects or tasks of a limited duration;

(g) Advisory Board – individuals selected by the president and approved by the board of directors to sit on the advisory board and provide advice to the company. Unlike the board of directors an advisory board has no authority in regard to the strategic direction or affairs of the company and therefore no corresponding responsibility;

(h) Professional Service Providers – examples include lawyers, accountants, bankers, investment bankers, engineers, executive search firms etc. These service providers are retained to provide periodic professional services to the company;

(i) Lenders – consists of those individuals or entities who loan funds to the entrepreneurial company; and

(j) Suppliers – consists of those individuals or entities who provide supplies of any nature whatsoever to the entrepreneurial company (i.e. raw material, equipment, tools, utilities, space etc.).

The entrepreneur should utilize his or her entire network and that of their current team to source additional team members. It is the best team that wins, not the best product in the biggest market.

Pitfall #7 Interview All Potential Team Members

Having acknowledged the importance of his or her team the entrepreneur must now build the very best team possible. Most entrepreneurs are accustomed to interviewing individuals for employment positions. However, legal counsel can greatly assist the entrepreneurial client by advising the entrepreneur to interview all potential team members and by recommending that the entrepreneur insist upon two "gating" characteristics without which the candidate should never be invited to join the company team. These two fundamental and non-negotiable characteristics are a strong interest in and work ethic for the entrepreneurial business and an ethically based character. Many authors and commentators speak of having a founder's "passion" for the entrepreneurial business, but in my view it is unreasonable to expect a non-founder to have the same passion for the business as a founder. However, it is reasonable to expect a team member to demonstrate a strong preference for entrepreneurial business ventures and to provide a resumé exhibiting a consistent and successful work ethic.

In terms of character, nothing can destroy or fatally wound a business more than consistently unethical behaviour demonstrated by team members, in particular those in key leadership and management positions. The corporate landscape is littered with examples of how insidious and irreparably destructive unethical leadership behaviour can be. All potential team members should be thoroughly interviewed, references requested and subsequently checked. In some appropriate cases independent investigatory services should be utilized. The entrepreneur should not be seeking team members who are in possession of a blemish free history, for such a standard is met by few. Rather, the entrepreneur should seek out those individuals who when faced with personally difficult or morally challenging decisions make the ethical choice 99 times out of 100.

Only after the entrepreneur is satisfied that these two fundamental and non-negotiable characteristics are present, should the entrepreneur turn to traditional interview precepts in hopes of revealing the candidates with the most appropriate experience and expertise for the team position in question.

Hard working but unethical team members cause decay and ultimately destroy companies, especially those which are embryonic and entrepreneurial.

Pitfall #8 Understand And Prepare For Due Diligence

Due diligence is the process by which third parties (i.e. financiers, acquirors and their professional services providers) pour over every aspect of a business. Entrepreneurs generally do not appreciate how thorough and intrusive this process will inevitably be. The analogy to envision is that due diligence in a business and legal context is the same as an autopsy in an unsolved murder investigation. No stone is left unturned and the entrepreneur will feel thoroughly violated by the time the process is complete. The entrepreneur should not expect otherwise.

Experienced legal counsel will prepare the entrepreneur for this process and lead him or her and the entrepreneur's team through it from start to finish. In this regard, the following recommendations are helpful to the entrepreneur:

(a) Run your business from day one as if the intensive due diligence process could begin tomorrow. Legal counsel can provide a reference framework and checklist for this process;

(b) Understand that a positive due diligence experience will enhance the third parties' appetite for the proposed transaction. However, know that a negative due diligence experience will almost always cause the third party to re-negotiate the proposed transaction and sometimes cause it to back out and cancel the transaction altogether;

(c) Make use of an electronic data site as early as possible. This data site should be populated with soft copies of all information and documentation described in the framework and checklist referred to in subparagraph (a) above. Access to the data site can be strictly controlled by the usual internet security measures. The advantages of an electronic data site are substantial, both for the company and those parties performing company due diligence. Desktop, laptop and pda 24/7 access, secure due diligence, ease of keeping company information and documentation current, speed of due diligence and long-term cost savings are but some of the advantages; and

(d) The entrepreneur should become familiar with all key information and documentation being provided through the due diligence process and should prepare commercially reasonable explanations and/or proposed solutions to respond to diligence deficiencies of which he or she is aware. Legal counsel will encourage full disclosure (although usually in a staged manner) and the entrepreneur should abide by this advice. Third parties do expect the due diligence process to reveal deficiencies in the company's business, but they do not expect concealment of those issues – concealment kills deals!

Working together the entrepreneur and legal counsel can turn an unpleasant and unavoidable process into one which increases company efficiency and effectiveness and also enhances a third party's appetite for a strategic company transaction.

Pitfall #9 Source And Accept Equity Funds Prudently

It is common for entrepreneurs to receive some modest seed financing from family and friends, but the equity funds which are fueling start-up and early stage technology companies in Canada today are primarily provided by angel investors, with some government program funding and venture capital injections. Angel investors are generally wealthy individuals who wish to utilize a small portion of their financial resources to invest in start-up or early-stage business opportunities. The following comments are intended to assist entrepreneurs in sourcing and closing angel investment.

Fundamentally important to the entrepreneur will be not only closing the amount of desired funding, but closing it with the angel or angels who most enhance the team which the entrepreneur is building (see Pitfall #7). When seeking equity funds entrepreneurs will usually receive advice from multiple sources, but regardless of the source it is a disciplined and structured approach to fundraising that will maximize the chances of raising the desired funds from the right angel investor. As experienced legal counsel in this field, we have acted for hundreds of those seeking and providing equity investment. Some of the recommendations that have stood the test of time in both boom and bust fundraising environments are as follows:

(a) The entrepreneur should prepare a summary of the business plan on fifteen pages or less covering the topics of technology (product/service), market, team, finances (request for funds/cash flow/ revenue model) and exit strategy. The summary should serve to excite and inform potential angel investors and must be available both in soft copy and as a slide deck for presentation purposes. Key members of the entrepreneur's team must review and sign off on the summary before it is provided to potential investors;

(b) Once finalized, the slide deck version of the business plan summary is to be presented to key team members and rehearsed until it can be articulated (not read) in no more than thirty exciting and informative minutes. This process will ensure as much as is reasonably possible that the "pitch" is comprehensive, consistent and exciting. This will in turn maximize the odds that each potential angel investor who receives the pitch for funding has their standard questions and concerns largely addressed prior to their raising them. This will permit the entrepreneur and potential angel investor to engage in a more customized and meaningful discussion about the possibility of an investment "fit"; and

(c) While the "pitch" is being perfected in (b) above, the appropriate team members should prepare a list of potential angel investors from the team's collective network and research. The team should endeavour to rank the potential investors from most likely to least likely to invest based upon their actual and acquired knowledge of the potential angel investor (i.e. history of investment in technology companies, preferred investment parameters, currently available investment funds etc.). The most appropriate team member will then approach the first ranked potential angel investor and arrange for execution of a non-disclosure agreement and delivery of a soft copy of the business plan summary. The objective is to arrange an opportunity to pitch the potential angel investor, commence discussions, move to due diligence and the preparation of legal documentation and to ultimately close an equity financing. Multiple potential angel investors are engaged until the desired equity financing is completed.

In our experience abiding by these recommendations will greatly assist in reducing the time required to raise equity funds and increase the chances of closing an acceptable financing from a team enhancing angel investor.

Pitfall #10 Document All Material Relationships and Transactions

Technology entrepreneurs pride themselves on being multi-taskers who are nimble and smart risk takers. Resources are few and speed is required to keep moving the business forward. However, legal counsel knows that notwithstanding the cliché, the devil is very much in the details. One verbal misunderstanding, confusing e-mail exchange or incomplete contract and the business can stall indefinitely as the entrepreneur attempts to resolve a misunderstanding which can quickly become a heated dispute with the opposite party. How do the technology entrepreneur and legal counsel resolve their differing perspectives to properly document important relationships and transactions in an effective, yet fast-paced manner?

Experienced legal counsel to technology entrepreneurs will recommend and happily adopt the following approach:

(a) Frequent communication by e-mail, voice mail and cell phone, and when necessary on a 24/7 basis;

(b) Acknowledgement by legal counsel that not all relationships and transactions will be thoroughly documented and a corresponding acknowledgement from the entrepreneur that he or she will discuss with legal counsel the need, or not, to document a relationship or a transaction before attempting to agree upon same with the other party;

(c) When legal counsel and the entrepreneur agree that a relationship or transaction does not require a custom-made and thorough papering, legal counsel will nevertheless advise the entrepreneur with respect to the use of standard form agreements, precedents, brief written accounts of the understanding or agreement reached between the entrepreneur and the other party or verbal discussions to be had;

(d) When legal counsel and the entrepreneur agree that formal and customized legal documentation is required, the entrepreneur will first provide a summary (preferably in writing i.e. e-mail) of the material deal points of the relationship or transaction and then permit legal counsel to draft a formal written agreement to be negotiated and executed between the parties. Legal counsel will provide, if possible, estimates of the time and legal costs associated with completing this exercise;

(e) Use of a team approach where the actions contemplated in (c) and (d) above can be commenced, and in certain cases completed, by individuals other than only the entrepreneur and the lead legal counsel; and

(f) Agreement to meet regularly to assess the communication and advisory process and discuss possible improvements to same.

Prudent documentation and efficiency need not be mutually exclusive objectives for the technology entrepreneur.

Key Take-away:

Working together, the optimistic entrepreneur and his or her cautious legal counsel can avoid ten of the most common legal pitfalls and thereby increase the entrepreneur's chances of success!

Tom Hunter

Tom Hunter is a partner in Gowlings' Waterloo office and practises in the area of corporate, commercial and technology law. He also serves as Co-Chair of the Firm's National Technology Law Practice Group.

His particular areas of focus include assisting entrepreneurs with start-up and growth oriented companies, mergers and acquisitions and all aspects of equity and debt financing.

Tom was lead Counsel in the creation of PixStream Incorporated in 1996 and led the divestiture transaction of PixStream to Cisco in 2000 for a sale price of C$550 million. He has also served as lead counsel for over $1 billion of profitable exits for high-tech clients.

Tom is the Past Chair of the Waterloo Region Catholic Schools Foundation, the Vice-Chair of the Board of Governors of St. Mary's General Hospital and Chair of St. Mary's Mission, Ethics & Quality Control Committee.

He is also actively involved with the Schlegel Centre for Entrepreneurship at Wilfrid Laurier University, and is a member of the Advisory Council for the Centre for Business, Entrepreneurship & Technology at the University of Waterloo.

People

Rod Foster

What have I learned in over 25 years of business? I have learned that there is one "thing" that can keep me up at night – people.

The majority of hurdles a new business faces can be overcome through creativity or a change in approach. In most instances, one is able to take a big problem, break it down, and solve it. Think about it: you can determine what your target market is; who your competition is; what your branding will be; what your product will sell for; and who will be on your board of directors. Even money is a hurdle that can be worked over, through and around, and the best part about money is you know how much you have and how long you need it to last. Money is tangible, concrete, and unemotional.

People are different. And people are your business.

First, choose your employees wisely. You get your idea off the ground and you need to hire your first employee. Finding and hiring the right individuals is the most important decision a leader can make. Hiring the right person gives you an adrenaline rush like no other. When you watch a team come together and accomplish a goal that they themselves thought was insurmountable, the feeling is remarkable. Individual and teams are what make your days exciting and fun.

I estimate it takes on average 90 days to find and secure a new employee. Most small organizations hire tactically – I need these things done and this is the skill set and experience that it requires. The fact is you are building a business and a team, and you need to define what that team will be. We post jobs that define skill sets, and typically include the bullet "must be a good team player". How do we define what the team looks like, and the type of person and personality that will make a "good team player"?

My mother used to say "you never know if someone is a true friend until you go through ¡#$% with them." True friends stand up and work with you to overcome life's hurdles. The same is true in business, and especially for start-up businesses. You need to determine whether or not applicants possess the skill set and traits for the business. The interview process is the time to do it, and in my experience, most employers do not take enough time digging in and asking the type of questions that will help to determine the applicant's true traits. Instead, they often spend the majority of time asking about accomplishments and how they achieved them. I want to know how the person approaches a new challenge, how do they handle stress? What about the conflicts they had with other people – how were those addressed and what was the outcome? In sports, it is often the unheralded players who take the spotlight in the tense moments of their sport. These players have the ability to focus and raise their level in stressful situations. In a start-up you will have more than your share of those moments were you will need your team's players to take the spotlight.

Employees will be your most considerable investment in time and money, yet most businesses only invest in training directly related to an employee's job function: technical training, sales training, marketing training. Why not invest the money up front, prior to hiring, by determining an applicant's personality skills through testing? The tests cost a few hundred dollars, but can objectively ensure you are making the best decision. It also allows you to consider fit with the team and the business: a team needs many skills, different ways of looking at things, different personalities. Each individual has a different way that they communicate – will their style be right in your environment? I have hired individuals who shine in the interview process and not so much in the day to day world. Remember, in most organizations, by the time a new employee understands the role, the culture, the way things are done you can easily be 12 months into your relationship. The cost if you make a poor decision is not insignificant. The reward if you get it right – you can spend more of your time focusing on productive initiatives.

Growing the business

Your business continues to grow over the next year. Some of the team members who were there a year ago have led the change, whereas others are struggling to keep up. Who gets the recognition and promotion to take on a new task? What if someone internally wants a promotion, yet there is a better candidate outside the organization – do you hire and potentially send the message that internal career growth is not available and risk losing employees? I have had that happen. I also have put people in positions when from a skill standpoint they had very little practical experience, and watched them thrive. Their attitude and aptitude was the game changer and led to their personal and the businesses success. What do you need, and who can do it? There is a saying never promote your best sales person to be the sales manager because the skills of a sales person are quite different than those of a manager, and sales people may not like administrative tasks– not being the hero in closing the deal. The goal is to put the best person in the right job. At one point in my career, I worked for a small company which was purchased by a large corporation. My peers had 20+ years experience in the company while I was three years out of University. They did not want me as head of marketing, but the General Manager of the business did. He gave me the job and some great advice – take each of the others out individually – break up the problem. I asked each person what I had to do to earn their respect, and 90 days to do it. And I promised to leave if I did not. The problem was not if I could do the job, the problem was would my peers let me. A year later they asked me to take over sales as well.

Invest in good staff

I have had the opportunity to work for individuals who trained me in the skills to become a more effective manager. How many start-ups and smaller organizations invest the time and money in what I would argue offers the highest intangible ROI they will make? How many hours do hockey players practice and get coached before they get their 15-20 minutes on the ice per game? Why do we not do the same in our business with our teams? In my business, we invest in outside training for new first time mangers. We also invest in all managers in areas like "how to coach for top performers". The most effective managers I have seen spend the majority of their time creating the environment for themselves and their team to be successful. They invest in hiring the right attitude and then teach the job. They are clear and concise in communicating the team's goals and each member's roles and responsibilities. They get out of the way and trust them to get it done; they watch, listen and manage through patterns and instinct; and they help when required. When these managers promote, they examine an employee's potential, with less emphasis on their history. As an example, in sports, a general manager has the choice to sign a veteran player at the twilight of a career who has a history of success or an up-and-coming player with all the skills the team needs although with only a few years of professional experience. A tough decision although I wager that most would take the younger player given their potential for years ahead. They look at the future potential more than the past.

You may not retain all good staff

Losing a key player as they move forward in their life with another organization can cause a sleepless night or a temporary loss of focus, but remember, no one person should be the business. The truth is that as an employer you "rent" people's minds. They can and will leave at some point to experience a new chapter in their lives and it often happens just when you think you have everything under control. Personally, I view this situation as an opportunity to initiate positive change, by giving a deserving employee 'the chance", or by hiring a true A level player with new ideas, thoughts and energy. You will not retain all employees – the art is to have the next batter ready and capable of stepping in.

Not all individuals will fit in the organization

At some point, you will meet an individual who does not fit in the business, perhaps because of personality, attitude or skill set. Determining the correct course of action given your responsibilities to all 'stakeholders' in the business can cause you to toss and turn at night. Conflict and disagreements between employees may work, as often different views and open discussion make for better decisions. However, once people lose respect for an individual or for each other, this is a very difficult situation to turn around. I have tried to "fix" relationships like this by mediation – it can be done although less than 50% of the time. Similarly, you may be faced with an employee who consistently shows poor judgment that impacts the business. While you may be reluctant to fire someone, most leaders will tell you that they tend to take too long to let this type of person go, and that this inadvertently caused them and other employees turmoil. In my experience, one must be diligent and act with great thought and care but delaying firing does not solve the issue. This situation has arisen in my business career several times; in almost every instance, at least one employee has commented that they felt better working for a company that holds people accountable. Mediocrity was not part of those businesses' culture.

Many years ago, one of the most successful advertising executives was asked why his company was the market leader. He replied, "Our greatest assets come up the elevator in the morning and go down the elevator at night". I urge you to think through what you want the culture of your business to be. Culture is created by the individuals working within the framework you establish, the individuals you hire, the individuals you promote. If you agree people are your business and your greatest asset then why not invest your time and resources proportionately? Most start-ups do not.

If you do, then I believe you will have many more good sleeps ahead of you.

Rod Foster

Rod leads Covarity's overall strategic direction and drives its commitment to world class solutions for the financial services market. Rod has over 25 years experience in software sales, marketing and operations with Ironside Technologies, Bay Networks, Crowntek, and GE Canada. Rod holds a Bachelor of Business Administration degree from Wilfrid Laurier University. In addition to serving as President and CEO of Covarity, Rod is a board member with the Better Business Bureau of Mid-Western and Central Ontario, is on the Board of Governors of the Grand River Hospital Foundation and is a member of the Accelerator Centre Advisory Council for start-up companies.

Outsourcing Made Possible

Cameron Hay

I made my first trip to China in the spring of 2003. Our company, Unitron Hearing, was in a process of renewal, and we had determined that we needed to move our manufacturing to Asia. While labour cost was a factor in the decision, like most high-tech companies, labour was actually a relatively small component of product cost and alone really couldn't justify the risks in quality, delivery and reputation that we were assuming by moving production out of the centre where it had been for four decades.

There were a number of other reasons to move to Asia, and in particular China. One of the most important reasons was not an obvious one. Unitron needed to focus our Canadian headquarters on our core competencies, which were R&D and global sales and marketing management. As long as manufacturing was in Canada, we tended to see ourselves as *manufacturers*. We had the culture of a company that had over half of its workforce "on-the-line". This culture influenced how executives spent our time, what kind of initiatives we worked on, and what we thought was important.

However, while we were competent manufacturers, it wasn't going to be the key to our competitiveness or our future. Our products are hearing aids. These little devices are actually digital-signal-processing computers, and the real competitive advantage Unitron has is our ability to design and market the smallest devices that can run the most advanced real-time signal-processing algorithms. It was also critical that we have the easiest to use fitting software that connects to the devices in audiologists' offices and allows them to program and customize each hearing aid to the unique needs of each patient they see.

Like so many other Waterloo-region based companies, our biggest single advantage we have is the fact that we have access to the best mathematics, computer science and engineering skills on the planet. And Unitron was developing a reputation within our industry for having incredibly powerful software… in many cases generations ahead of our competitors. Yet the culture of being a manufacturer was so strong that in 2003 we kept our software engineers outside our building – in a portable unit that didn't even have washrooms!

Transforming the culture of the business from being *manufacturing* based to *high-tech* based was the largest catalyst to moving our production to Asia. There were other reasons... the supply chain of electronics components tended to be Asian-based. As we looked at our growth prospects, it was clear that we needed to develop a scaleable production platform that could grow three or four times larger, and it seemed far more strategic to build this platform in Asia rather than in Canada. And I knew enough about China to know that you can't do business in China without *being* in China.

The interesting thing about spring 2003 was that it was at the height of the global SARS outbreak. It's easy to forget the economic fears that went along with this health crisis, but at the time, it seemed crazy to many people to invest in China... after all, it was at the epicentre of the crisis, and it wasn't clear how or if it was going to end. I certainly wasn't going to make anyone go to China during this period, and therefore resolved to go myself – knowing that I may need to go into quarantine when I returned to Canada – to protect my family and my colleagues at Unitron from whatever I might bring back.

I flew from Toronto to Shanghai in May 2003 in a mostly empty plane, with my N95 masks in my carry-on. I wasn't sure what to expect, and was surprised to see how normal and crowded the Shanghai airport seemed to be. The surprise turned to shock when I faced a fearful customs inspector who was worried about my health. As he hastened to put on his mask, he informed me in all seriousness that Toronto was a hot-zone in the global SARS outbreak, whereas Shanghai did not have a single case. After some discussions, he allowed me into the country, but only on the condition that I have my temperature taken 4 times a day, I keep a log of everyone I saw, and that this logbook along with the temperature readings had to be turned into the hotel manager every evening. He also advised me that if I did develop a fever, I would be placed in a temporary "hospital" and be unable to fly home until I was given an all-clear. Yikes!

Once on the ground in Shanghai, the possibilities of China opened up to me. As one of only a few foreign companies investing in China at that time, I was offered turn-key solutions – everything from HR services to ready-built factories, tax holidays and incentives. After conducting appropriate due diligence, I elected to establish our manufacturing centre in the city of Suzhou – about two hours outside of Shanghai. I picked a location in a Singaporean-run *Export Processing Zone*, which was designed for companies like ours – stable, high quality manufacturing infrastructure with most products re-exported to North America and Europe.

By September, our product lines were up and running, and by the following spring we had virtually all our production in China. I never developed a fever, and by the end of the summer, the entire world was breathing a sigh of relief as SARS was waning. In fact, there was a rebound effect as thousands of companies flocked back to China in the fall of 2003, and certainly none of them received the levels of personal attention I received by going there when others wouldn't.

We were very positively surprised at the high levels of quality we achieved very quickly. Within the first few months, the quality at our Chinese facility exceeded that of our Canadian factory, and in the subsequent seven years we have never had a significant quality incident from our Chinese facility. The key for us is that we manage the factory ourselves… we haven't outsourced to local subcontractors, and we maintain our own quality standards along with hiring and training processes.

The transition in Canada was not easy. There were implications to our decision… we downsized our Canadian operations group by over 90%. It was hard to say goodbye to colleagues that had been with Unitron for a very long time. It was a difficult cultural change for the organization, and difficult for many people to accept – especially because we were downsizing at the same time we were experiencing unprecedented growth.

The most challenging part of the transition was asking Canadian manufacturing personnel to train their new Chinese colleagues and set up the processes and systems in China that very clearly would lead to the downsizing in Canada. It was an awkward situation, but basically unavoidable, as there was no other way to ramp up the capabilities and knowledge in China. We were as open as we could be, and asked for volunteers from our Canadian group to help with the transition. We were concerned about potentially destructive behaviour during this period, but generally people continued to work in a highly professional manner, even when it was clear that their jobs were likely going to end. The key at that time was being very open about what was happening and why, and allowing people to retain their dignity during this period. Perhaps not surprisingly, the people that volunteered to actively help in the transition were generally the ones that stayed on after the downsizing in our prototyping and early-volume production lines that remained in Canada. We resolved to treat all the people we had to let go very fairly. After all, these people were hard working, effective and loyal. While we were changing our manufacturing approach, they still needed and deserved to be treated with respect.

For staff in other departments, the change was less traumatic for obvious reasons – they were not directly affected by the downsizing and could see the immediate benefit. The software engineers were most delighted when we brought them back into the main building from their portable offices. Marketing and Sales were concerned about the implications of a "Made in Canada" story being changed to a "Made in China" story, but as we were far from the first company to make this change, it proved to be a minor issue.

We discovered the necessity to be far more disciplined in our product development and ramp-up processes. When manufacturing was no longer in the same building as engineering and in fact was not on the same continent, we needed to increase the formalization of process instructions, engineering changes, and work instructions. We discovered that many of our products were made with undocumented processes that often came verbally from process engineering to the shop floor. By increasing the disciplines of communication and documentation between engineering and manufacturing, we found quality and consistency improved – there were far fewer assumptions about how things were done, and far more effort put into defining all aspects of workflow, process, controls, and quality standards.

The other implication to having manufacturing off-shore is ensuring design engineers remain fully knowledgable of the characteristics of manufacturing processes. When mechanical designers do not have direct access to the factory in which their designs will be built, there can be a dangerous loss of awareness of process capabilities – especially in high volume production. We invest a lot of effort in regular two-way knowledge transfer between the design site and manufacturing site. We also retain a "stabilization" line in Canada that has identical processes to those in China. This line is used during the initial volume ramp-up of production, and only when the production is proving stable at higher volumes will the product be transferred to China.

I remain convinced that the change was necessary, and in fact had we not made this radical departure from our past, Unitron would likely have struggled to transform itself into a leader in our field. At a personal level and as a proud Canadian, I really struggled with the implications of this decision. But the change did allow us to focus on what we do best – today Unitron is the most innovative and creative company in our industry, and was recent winner of the Premier's Catalyst Award for Company with the Best Innovation. The manufacturing area has been transformed into the hub of our ever expanding R&D centre, and in fact we are close to having the same number of people on-staff that we had before the change. Today's workforce in Canada is comprised of engineers, scientists and professionals. Our culture is strong, and our employees are some of the most engaged in Canada, as our placement as one of Canada's Best Small/Medium Employers has shown.

Unitron has always had a global outlook – even as a relatively small company, we have considered the entire world as our market. The move of manufacturing to China was the most radical of our international investments and it further cemented our perspective that we can and will be successful competing at a global level. In 2003 we had sales offices in three countries – Canada, US and Germany. Today Unitron has sales offices in over 18 countries and our products are dispensed in an additional 54 markets through independent distributors. Being a Canadian company garners goodwill on every continent, and following through with world-class technology is a winning combination for success.

Focus matters. Our Canadian organization is our creativity and innovation centre. We needed to make sure this organization could be the best in the world in this mission, and that meant we needed to stop doing things that were a distraction and/or not a competitive advantage

Timing is everything. We went to China at a time when no-one else was going. This decision gave us access to resources that our company would never otherwise have had access to, and allowed us to go from first visit to in-production in less than 4 months.

Do it yourself. I personally went to oversee the factory in China. While it wasn't a core competency in Canada, the implications of a screw-up were enormous, especially if it led to poorer quality or missed customer commitments. I simply couldn't delegate this risk. Further, the decision to go at the height of SARS made it mandatory that only I go. The organization saw the importance of the change, and generally got behind it quickly, because I was at the front-line.

Be Open. This change had serious implications for many people in our organization. Rather than hide these implications or pretend nothing would change, we decided to tell people the truth, and kept them informed throughout this time. We didn't try to spin the truth. It wasn't always easy, but it helped the people affected come to terms with the change.

Invest in your Culture. A change as significant as the one we went through has significant implications on company culture. We thought through the culture we wanted at the end of the change, and actively worked towards shifting the attitudes and behaviours at the workplace towards this culture.

Cameron Hay

Cameron is an Executive in Residence at Communitech, where he acts as an advisor to early stage technology companies. Cameron joined Unitron in 2002 as COO and was President & CEO from 2004 to 2010. Unitron is a Kitchener-based company in the field of hearing healthcare with sales in 70 countries around the world. Cameron joined Unitron in 2002 from Cap Gemini Ernst & Young, where he was a management consultant in the areas of strategy and supply chain, with a focus on high technology. Cameron started his career at IBM Canada and Celestica Inc. as a Process Engineer. Cameron has a Bachelor of Science in Engineering from the University of Manitoba and an MBA from the Richard Ivey School of Business at the University of Western Ontario.

PART III
MAKING IT HAPPEN

Guardian Capital is a proud supporter of Canadian Entrepreneurs and The Entrepreneurial Effect (Waterloo)

GUARDIAN CAPITAL
ADVISORS LP

PRIVATE WEALTH MANAGEMENT GROUP

Guardian Capital Group Limited

Since 1962, Guardian Capital Group Limited and its subsidiaries have built one of Canada's leading independent wealth management organizations. Our basic principles are innovation and prudence.

Guardian Capital Group Limited

Commerce Court West
199 Bay St. Suite 3100, Toronto, Ontario
www.guardiancapital.com

The Innovation Centre and Entrepreneurship Development in Waterloo

Josie Graham

The words "entrepreneur" and "technology" seem to be linked in many people's minds to the many world-class Waterloo-based companies: RIM, DALSA (now Teledyne DALSA), OpenText, and many others. How did Waterloo become synonymous with innovation? Part of this can be attributed to University of Waterloo's (UW) unique role in the community but what other policies, associations and institutions led to such an innovative community? Reviewing history, methods and processes may help other communities and organizations wishing to duplicate that success.

"The University of Waterloo should give serious consideration to the establishment of an innovation program."[1] – C. Frank Phripp, Director, Waterloo Research Institute (UW) 1975.

Phripp's cautious recommendation followed a conference that July on "Technology Transfer via Entrepreneurship" sponsored by Carnegie-Mellon University, MIT (Massachusetts Institute of Technology) and the University of Oregon.

In the 1960s and 1970s the research administration at UW had the foresight and vision to emphasize not only the generation of new technologies through research, but also the application of them for profit in the Canadian and international economies. Thus, they introduced new policies on campus to stimulate and arouse faculty interest in the commercial application and licensing of developed technologies. The University was already a pioneer in fostering industrial links through the student co-operative program, and the direct support of additional industrial objectives was a logical extension.

In 1968, the Federal Department of Industry, Trade and Commerce (ITC), now known as Industry Canada, launched the Industrial Research Institute through the University's contract research services.

---

[1]   The Start-up and Development of an Innovation Centre", Canadian Innovation Centre, 1985

Progress appeared slow, but in hindsight these small steps were giant leaps forward. There was a culture of being extremely cautious in the protection of academic purity at a time when "Many projects were frustrated because of incomplete mechanisms to bridge the gulf between conception of an innovative technology and its profitable appearance in the marketplace."[2] Thus began UW's quest for a more comprehensive solution to the "application" problem. A major study was undertaken of universities in the US and Europe facing similar issues, but particularly in the US, where the Bayh-Dole Act of 1980[3] gave universities unfettered rights to inventions resulting from federally-funded research. Those findings revealed that a new mechanism was required which would provide not "piecemeal but comprehensive support to the practical application of any form of innovative technology." [4] This new mechanism would be profit-inspired and operate independently, although associated with the university. This new mechanism would be labelled an "Innovation Centre".

For successful creation, such a comprehensive centre needed to have access to adequate resources. Experiments elsewhere established that unless this centre could provide access to a wide range of capabilities backed by adequate investment, chances for success would be slim. "A critical mass phenomenon was evident. While this conclusion was clear, the path to establish the Centre was not. The marketing of this institutional innovation was fraught with the same difficulties faced by the technology application problem it was intended to solve!"[5] There were many issues to be overcome – many still seem familiar today. Few within the academic community saw the need for such an organization. Many feared the loss of their academic freedom or the rights to their research. Many in industry were puzzled as to why such an organization was needed and were sceptical. In the end, all conceded that *IF* it could be done anywhere, it would be at the University of Waterloo.

Braving these difficulties and challenges, in 1975 the University of Waterloo created the Innovation Centre. It was opened piecemeal in April 1976 with the Inventor's Assistance Program and with the support of $15,000 from the Canadian Patents and Development Limited. The program attracted the attention of inventors but the Centre soon found

---

2 *Ibid*
3 Bayh–Dole Act or University and Small Business Patent Procedures Act, Title 35 U.S.C 200-212, 37 CFR 401, Dec. 12, 1980; US legislation dealing with intellectual property arising from federal government-funded research.
4 The Start-up and Development of an Innovation Centre", Canadian Innovation Centre, 1985
5 *Ibid*

an immediate challenge. Opting for bigger opportunities in the US, inventors would not invest "even a small fee for deliberate systematic investigation of the worth of their invention". Yet, in spite of this, the use of the Centre's services grew steadily; however, not to the level of being self-sustaining. In the 10 years from 1975 to 1985, the Centre helped 7,000 inventors, assessed 2,200 inventions for commercial viability, set up agreements with 61 of them to help them commercialize their invention, and saw the start-up of 39 companies creating 139 jobs. All was possible through a five year grant of up to $1M per year from ITC's Technology Outreach Program (TOP) which ran from 1981 and was renewed twice – in 1986 and again in 1991.

At the same time much specialized needs were identified: an Engineering Computer Software Development and Distribution Service and a Chemical Process Development Service. As specialized divisions, they were brought in under the Innovation Centre umbrella which in so doing drew in much needed faculty support. The business aspect of innovation activities began to lead to discussions with Wilfrid Laurier University and York University but, with it came an excessive bureaucratic burden that would prove to be beyond the value of the co-institutional arrangements. It also confirmed the earlier conclusion that a totally independent business operation was the best structure for the proposed Innovation Centre.

As the Centre evolved through 1976 and 1977, Federal government recognition of the contribution of small business to the economy grew to the point that UW's advocacy of an Innovation Centre being the catalyst for the creation of small business came to be heard by the policy advisors of the Federal Department of Industry Trade & Commerce (ITC). The well-received message led to the writing of a discussion paper by E. L. Holmes, C. Frank Phripp and E. Rhodes in July of 1977 which was followed by a meeting held at ITC in September where the concept was thoroughly examined. The discussion paper included a review of the various initiatives existent at UW and it put forward a proposal that would build on these initiatives using the experiences of innovation centres in the US to establish the University of Waterloo Innovation Centre. The proposal clearly recognized two important points: the value of small business to a nation's economy and the desire of Federal and Provincial governments to support good, small-business ventures.

The proposed University of Waterloo Industrial Innovation Centre would act in the following areas:

- Transferring university research into the business sector
- Expanding the existing evaluation service for the private sector
- Developing a chemical pilot process facility for use by small companies and university researchers

- Seeing the creation of an engineering software development and distribution service; and
- Assisting entrepreneurs through programs that prepared them to advance their business ideas through support from an incubator facility

Waterloo's Industrial Innovation Centre was envisioned as being a separate corporate entity with a Board of Directors representing industry, government and the University of Waterloo. Originally it was to be wholly owned by UW with close operational ties between the Centre's programs and the appropriate UW facilities.

The discussion paper spurred much conversation within the Federal and Provincial governments and also within the University and, on March 20, 1978 a formal proposal was prepared. The intent was to interest the Federal government in supporting the establishment of Waterloo's Innovation Centre whose objective would be "to supplement the role of the University of Waterloo in serving society, particularly to benefit the economy by productive application of new knowledge acquired from indigenous research or elsewhere.[6] The proposal included a plan to expand the Inventors Assistance Program to include invention development, the need for entrepreneurial training, the payment via royalties or equity for services and the need to evaluate ideas early in their life. In that proposal, the processing of an innovative idea as intended and practised by the Centre, would see an investment that would begin at a high level and least be costly, perhaps leading to more in-depth, more costly evaluations and, would see a succession of Go/No-Go decisions that would be applied to projects. All ideas presented would have a hearing and an unbiased response.

In June 1978 three things happened. Then Minister of State for Science and Technology, Mr. Judd Buchanan announced a government decision to establish up to five university-based Industrial Research and Innovation Centres. Ontario Minister of Colleges and Universities, Dr. Harry Parrot gave support in principle and Dr. B.C. Matthews, President of UW announced the intention of the University to establish the Industrial Innovation Centre. This activity sparked enthusiasm amongst other Ontario universities to ask UW to form a consortium to "do the job right". Given UW's experience of trying to engage with Wilfrid Laurier and York, the invitation was declined. The consortium went forward but failed to garner the support of Queen's Park or Ottawa, and the effort was abandoned. Although very much interested in the Centre's activities, the Ontario government chose to independently fund these types of activities through the creation of the IDEA Corporation and the

---

[6] Ibid

BILD[7] program. Nevertheless, Ontario support for UW's Centre was ultimately achieved by the presence of an Assistant Deputy Minister on the Centre's Board and a collaborative arrangement with the IDEA Corporation for invention evaluation and development.

In April 1979, the Federal support announced in June 1978 was confirmed. The government would provide École Polytechnique de Montréal[8] and UW each with a $200,000 start-up grant to establish an Industrial Innovation Centre at their respective institutions. The agreement for start-up was signed in September 1979 whereupon the Centre's name was changed from Waterloo Industrial Innovation Centre to Ontario Industrial Innovation Centre to comply with Ottawa having five regional centres. Start-up was long and it took until March 1981 to be truly operational. During this time the Centre continued to do its work. It was able to survive by being within the University's "womb". When the Centre formally launched in March 1981 in an off-campus facility, the name was changed again. This time from the Ontario Industrial Innovation Centre to the Canadian Industrial Innovation Centre/Waterloo to ensure that there was no confusion as to which government was funding the venture. An important component of the Centre's activities at the time, were two programs for students – one to facilitate their innovative activities and the other to obtain hands-on student assistance in assessing and developing innovations for the Centre's clients. These programs provided students with the knowledge and skills necessary to help them bring innovations and ideas to market-readiness. In recognition of the contributions to Canada's innovation community, the Centre was awarded the Manning Innovation Award in 1982; this was the first time this award had been given to an organization, rather than an innovator.

Using the experience and knowledge gained, the Centre developed a number of tools. One was a Venture Validation service to efficiently counsel entrepreneurs and help hundreds of them evaluate their busi-

---

7   "Building Ontario in the 1980s, January 27, 1981", Ontario Board of Industrial Leadership, 1981, Ontario Board of Industry Leadership and Development (BILD) established in January 1981: $1.2B over 5 years to develop import replacement and export potential to improve Ontario's trade balance, technological development, training and job creation; allocation of $100M to hi-technology development program in 5 areas – advanced manufacturing, microelectronics, automotive parts, resource machinery and farm equipment.

8   École Polytechnique de Montréal, http://www.polymtl.ca/rensgen/en/toutPoly/enBref/index.php founded in late 1800's; main purpose until 1960s was to train engineers; then the focus turned to research; it remains a leading research institution in applied sciences.

ness concepts and bring them into the marketplace. Over the years this service became the Market Preview Plus (MPP) then later the MEV, the Market Evaluation Validation. The MEV process is best explained by what the Centre today calls the Pre-Revenue Innovation Commercialization Modality™ (PRICM). The modality recognizes that taking a new product from concept through to sustainable commercial success involves a number of steps, in a certain sequence. While each given specific situation is unique and the commercialization effort must be tailored and personalized to suit, the methodology is valid and repeatable. The PRICM lays out a sequence of four pre-revenue stages for any innovation based on 42 Critical Factors determined by the Centre's years of research as being the issues every entrepreneur needs to address for venture success. Each of these stages has a focus and intent that put the issues into perspective and sequence. More importantly, each stage closes with a commitment and an understanding to go forward, pause or retreat and adjust, or to stop and they answer the questions of why, what, where and how. This is followed ultimately by a post-revenue stage that addresses the inevitable stall of an innovation when one or more of the pre-revenue stages was skipped or was based on fundamentally incorrect data or assumption (Figure 2).

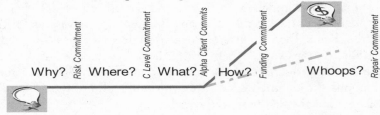

Figure 2: Asking the right question at the right time

This four-staged approach to being market-ready is characterized by a critical path which the Centre calls the Commercialization Roadmap or, more appropriately "pecuniarization" where new innovations proceed through a number of stages on their path to become commercial successes. Pecuniarization is the process of taking a novel idea or business concept and turning it into a thing of value which people will pay money for.

At each "way point" towards pecuniarization, there are critical challenges, each requiring focused attention and specialized resources. For entrepreneurs, the ability to identify which stage they are at and obtain the appropriate assistance can shorten the path to market, reduce their likelihood of making a bad decision and increase their likelihood for commercial success. The pathway to pecuniarize an idea or business concept is illustrated in Figure 3.

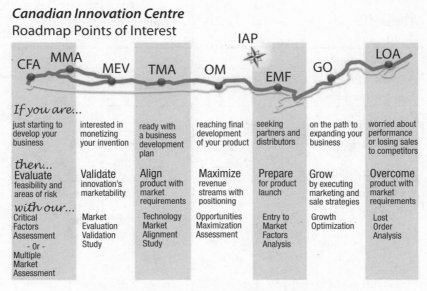

Canadian Innovation Centre
Roadmap Points of Interest

CFA	MMA	MEV	TMA	OM	IAP	EMF	GO	LOA

If you are...

just starting to develop your business	interested in monetizing your invention	ready with a business development plan	reaching final development of your product	seeking partners and distributors	on the path to expanding your business	worried about performance or losing sales to competitors

then...

Evaluate feasibility and areas of risk	**Validate** innovation's marketability	**Align** product with market requirements	**Maximize** revenue streams with positioning	**Prepare** for product launch	**Grow** by executing marketing and sale strategies	**Overcome** product with market requirements

with our...

Critical Factors Assessment - Or - Multiple Market Assessment	Market Evaluation Validation Study	Technology Market Alignment Study	Opportunities Maximization Assessment	Entry to Market Factors Analysis	Growth Optimization	Lost Order Analysis

Figure 3: CIC Pecuniarization Roadmap

In 1997/8 using the principles embedded in the Centre's validation and alignment studies, the Centre performed a study to determine the potential market acceptance and usability testing for a wireless email device. That email device was the Blackberry. Some of the recommendations from that study are still evident in today's selection of product offerings from RIM. The methodology used then is still used today to bring many innovative technology products into the market place.

The introduction of a market evaluation/validation process into the commercialization path can reduce the likelihood of failure. Further, by adopting a formal market evaluation process, which the innovator does not bias, can increase both the likelihood of success and return on investment. Research into the effectiveness of a formal market evaluation process provides evidence of effectiveness. Research has shown that for opportunities where entrepreneurs validated their market opportunity, 70% of them were successful within five years, while only 18% were successful if they did not conduct a validation study (Figure 4). Further, a market evaluation study identifies fatal business flaws that help the entrepreneur identify what to fix, or even whether to proceed or not.

Market Evaluation theme	Clients who successfully commercialized	Clients who struggle to commercialize	Clients who did not commercialize
Validated the market	70%	18%	0%
Aligned the innovation to the market	100%	39%	0%
Pursued the customer's voice	60%	14%	0%
Understood their competitive position	70%	21%	0%
Formalized their marketing strategy	73%	39%	0%

Figure 4: The link between market evaluation and
successful commercialization of an idea

Traditional market research is done by large companies to provide evidence for them to use internally to justify the market opportunity they wish to attack. It is often concerned with existing markets, determining market segmentation and the size and trends in that market space. Further, market research is often undertaken independently of the innovation being proposed, and it can also be carried out retrospectively to confirm the effectiveness of launch strategy. This approach however is not as useful to new ventures which create new markets as was the case with RIM or if the focus is on a small market segment. Research in a situation like RIM's is market evaluation where it takes a bottom-up approach to validate the presence of a new market and to provide insights as to the most appropriate way to exploit the opportunity.

Market validation uses interviews with market stakeholders to answer specific market evaluation questions that help the innovator confirm the opportunity and approach first (and sometimes second or third) potential customers. Identifying, attracting and obtaining these initial customers are critical to the long term success of the business. Undertaking market evaluation is a formal process that involves disclosing specific (but sometimes limited) information about the innovation to validate market assumptions in the business plan, and sometimes make the necessary changes that might facilitate success. Six fundamental questions answered by market evaluation are:

Do customers in the target market see value in the proposed innovation?

Do the pricing, and proposed features and benefits, meet customer expectations (and provide a significant benefit over competitor solutions)?

What would be the first application of the product/service?

What is the purchasing process for acquiring this type of product or service?

Are there organizations that would be interested in promoting the product or service?

Are there adjacent markets which offer greater potential than the original envisaged market?

The Centre's process of undertaking market validation provides detailed answers to innovation-specific questions that help to identify initial market segments, how purchase decisions are made, distribution channels selected and product pricing, features and benefits decided. Correctly interpreted, this feedback can provide guidance on market potential and evolution, and ultimately whether the innovation can form the basis of a new venture. It provides valuable insights that enhance the dialogue between entrepreneurs and funders, advisors and researchers, to make better informed decisions; thus fulfilling the vision of a mechanism that would help turn the research into an application of the research for profit.

The Go/No-Go decision processes developed in the early days of the Centre emerged as the world renowned Stage-Gate™ product development process developed by Bob Cooper who served as the Centre's Director of Research, although he was based at McMaster University. The Centre has evolved the Go/No-Go into a new process called Inno-gate. Inno-Gate™ follows the Stage-Gate™ approach, but is designed to help organizations adopt process, service, and business model innovations into a company, based on input from all functional areas – production and operations, finance and, sales and marketing. The introduction of an Inno-Gate™ process requires the company to adopt the tools of quality management, product management, process management and change management.

A third tool developed was the Critical Factors Assessment (CFA), which still lies at the heart of many of the Centre's programs. The CFA is a proven assessment process which has been used to evaluate over 20,000 ideas. Independent research conducted by the University of Toronto measured a Venture Capitalist's ability to pick winners at 40%. This same study rated the Centre's ability at 79% using the Critical Factors Assessment tool.[9] The Center's CFA is a diagnostic tool to help

---

[9]   "Assessing the Commercial Viability of Seed- and Early Stage Ven-

entrepreneurs identify serious issues, manage those risks and address critical flaws while being a formal evaluation which could be shared with third parties interested in partnering with the venture. The five key factors which contribute to the validity of the tool are:

Process: Use of a proven standardized tool in the evaluation process increases the likelihood that all factors pertaining to the ultimate success of the innovation are considered. This allows evaluators to step through each factor, and not ignore one that they feel is unimportant. Experience has shown the Centre that each of the factors is pertinent in the decision making process.

Independent Third Party Validation: Whilst the innovators are the lead drivers in taking the product to market, their ability to influence the direction of market research and their selection of third party interactions often distorts objectivity. By removing the direct contact between the innovator and the assessor, the CFA produces a more objective view which is enhanced by the Peer Review.

Peer Review: Once the data from the innovator is entered and interpreted and the other data sources considered, the recommendations from the Centre's Business Analyst are taken to a peer review process for validation. This in-depth resource enhances the validity of the assessment undertaken, and increases its objectivity.

Case load: The centre has undertaken more than 20,000 studies and established processes to rapidly complete assessments. The recommendations made and the market potential identified, are compared to the database of opportunities evaluations that the Centre maintains.

Triangulation Review Process: Data for the Critical Factors Assessment (CFA) is taken from three important sources, each providing a significantly different perspective on the opportunity. First is the innovator who completes a 20 question disclosure document (not directly linked to the actual individual factors). Second, and as appropriate, third party stakeholders, such as board members, technology transfer officers or IRAP Industry Technology Advisors complete a revised commentary, based on the input from their original survey of the opportunity. Third, the Center's Analysts use their knowledge, experience, access to market studies, previous CFA studies and independent experts to prepare a draft assessment which is peer reviewed and then a final report with recommendations prepared.

Like the Venture Validation and the Go-No Go processes established by the Centre in the 1980's, the CFA is still used today. "It (the CFA)

---

tures", Dr. Thomas Astebro, The Journal of Private Equity – Strategies and Techniques for Venture Investing, Winter 2002, www.iijpe.com

does provide a great improvement over current practice in the screening of seed- and early-stage investments.... If the hit rate is maintained by VCs using the model, it would suggest a doubling of the rate of return on VCs' investments on seed- and early-stage investments due to the improvement in screening ability"[10] states Thomas Asteboro of the University of Toronto.

Turning back to the early 1980's, in collaboration with a US-based non-profit organization[11] the Centre launched the Entrepreneurship Institute of Canada to organize community forums across Canada that would help create jobs by networking local resources to serve local entrepreneurs. Today the networking is epitomized by Canada's Technology Triangle (CTT)[12] which was established in 1987, Communitech[13] in 1997 and most recently in October 2010, Canada's Digital Media Centre, more commonly known as the Hub[14]. The Accelerator Centre (AC)[15] at the David Johnston Research and Technology Park

---

[10] Ibid
[11] The Entrepreneurship Institute (1976), Columbus OH , http://www.tei.
      net/about.asp
[12] CTT Canada's Technology Triangle, http://www.techtriangle.
      com/about_canada's_technology_triangle_inc, not for profit, public/
      private economic development partnership consisting of 6 municipalities
      and corporate partners representing Waterloo Region.
[13] Communitech, a portmanteau of "Community" and "Technology",
      http://www.communitech.ca/about/start-here-communitech-101/histo-
      ry/ ; started as the Atlas Group to later become Waterloo Area Technol-
      ogy Association in 1997 with the support of 40 founding companies. The
      Atlas Group was comprised of:
      Yvan Couture, The TAAZ Group,
      Tom Jenkins, DALSA
      Ron Neumann, Maplesoft
      Ian McPhee, Watcom
      Jim Balsillie, RIM
      Peter Schwartz, Descartes
      John Branch, OpenText
      Randall Howard, MKS
      Steve Spicer, Spicer
      Doug Beynon
      Jim Estill
[14] Communitech Hub, http://www.communitechhub.ca/– opened Oct 7,
      2010; an open concept "sandbox" bringing together early stage digital
      media start-ups, enterprise companies, government and academic or-
      ganizations;
[15] Accelerator Centre, http://www.acceleratorcentre.com/about

which opened in 2006 is a 21st Century version of yesterday's incubator that cultivates technology. It is a place where entrepreneurs are able to accelerate the creation, growth, and development of their ideas into sustainable new technology companies and also promotes commercialization of research and technology rising out of all academic institutions in the Region of Waterloo. The Canadian Industrial Innovation Centre/Waterloo is now the Canadian Innovation Centre (CIC), having changed its name again in 1997.

The introduction of additional tools on-line and a soon to be launched web-based learning program in conjunction with the University of Toronto (School of Continuing Studies) and other partners is envisioned to make the CIC's website the "Go To" destination for innovators and entrepreneurs. Notably, CIC processes, in abbreviated forms, and personnel were used to prepare entrepreneurs for CBC TV's Dragons' Den television show about entrepreneurs.

In summary, Waterloo and the Canadian Innovation Centre succeeded in developing technology entrepreneurship based on a university which took such development very seriously, by creating, using and proving a series of evaluative processes: idea, venture and entrepreneur validation, marketing evaluation and commercialization development. One entrepreneurial success is difficult. A community or organizational track record of successes requires methods which are both innovative and which adapt to changing market conditions. Waterloo and the CIC could be a good model for other communities to adapt to their needs.

Josie Graham,

COO and Director Projects & Studies, Canadian Innovation Centre

Josie joined the Canadian Innovation Centre in 2003, after founding Strategic Advantages in 1999, a niche consulting firm focusing on new business development which Josie still operates. At the Centre, she provides Business Planning and Market Entry strategies to entrepreneurs, and has conducted over 100 Market Evaluation Validation Reports and Alignment studies. As a Business Advisor, she has been back many times to help entrepreneurs appearing on CBC TV's Dragons' Den television show. In her 25 years in business and 10 years of solutions selling in the high tech sectors, and as founder and CEO of Strategic Advantages, Josie's varied experience includes conducting Customer Satisfaction Index surveys for JD Powers' automotive clients, managing a small call centre specializing in lead generation for hi-tech companies, successfully promoting a N. American and European seminar series for one of them. She has managed operations, acted as the information gatekeeper for Business Development Consortium projects, being instrumental in helping an alternative fuel company take their licensed-in technology and business concept to market by creating the plan and the tools needed to get it there. Other experiences include building image and corporate identity, taking the lead on the market analysis for a major Canadian Medical office management software provider allowing them to retain their position as the largest medical office management provider in Ontario and helping client companies gain that edge for a strategic advantage. She has developed winning sales teams and established sales channels for a Waterloo-based mathematical software company in Europe, Latin America and the Asia Pacific regions. In the Business Development Department at Sparton Electronics, Josie played a key role as the company moved from a defense contractor to contract manufacturing. She is multilingual and a graduate from Glendon College, York University with Marketing studies from University of Western Ontario's Ivey School of Business, and Economic Development from the University of Waterloo.

The Keys to Social Entrepreneurship

Mike Morrice

In founding **Sustainable Waterloo** over the past several years, our over-arching challenge – as is the case for many entrepreneurs and start-up organizations – has been in not just building an organization or particular service offering, but in engaging a community of supporters from all sectors.

On a personal level, the need to engage supporters had an embedded challenge: I had to align my views of entrepreneurship with the needs of Waterloo Region's business community. My ideas went beyond just economic value-creation or profit maximization, to include the belief that the economy should serve the needs of society and the natural environment in which we operate. For me then, entrepreneurship was and is still about the pioneering of new ideas and solving tough problems with new thinking, but with the goal being to achieve some measure of social change. I've come to learn that this broader definition of entrepreneurship – one that is focused on finding a financially viable solution to a social problem – is aptly called social entrepreneurship.

Within this lens then, I was motivated to bring together people from a variety of backgrounds to jointly buy into a new idea in Waterloo Region.

The early success I have had in building this sort of "community of support" around **Sustainable Waterloo** comes from following five simple practices:
- Build long-standing relationships
- Include people in the process of change
- Collaborate across all sectors
- Leverage existing models, while taking risks to adapt as needed
- Provide supporters with a menu of options to contribute

These practices have been paramount to our early success in building a community around the work of Sustainable Waterloo. They have helped to transform the organization from an idea our team was deeply passionate about, to one that people across Waterloo Region have started to value.

First, is the need to move away from the transactional nature of many business relationships. I'm amazed by how pervasive this approach remains. Intuitively it is sensible that time spent nurturing long-term relationships is time well spent. At Sustainable Waterloo, be it when it comes to employees, volunteers, Board members, investors, or clients – really anyone with a level of interest in our work – the most vital part of it all has been an earnest desire to build trust and respect with each individual. Ultimately, these high-value relationships are what move the organization ahead in both its short and long-term goals.

Reflecting on our first six months, I can honestly say that without the support of five key people during that time we never would have made it past our first few thousand dollars of funding. They were champions of our work from the start, and they continue to be champions of ours today. If I had approached these individuals two years ago with a narrow focus on our immediate need to acquire funding, it's likely Sustainable Waterloo would have only benefited from a one-time injection of funds. Instead, these leaders have made critical connections for the organization, they've donated their time as Board members, some have provided funding, and others have provided in-kind services. The commonality between these five supporters is that their involvement has provided a sense of fulfilment for each, in each case time was spent at the outset building trust before making a particular Sustainable Waterloo-related request, and each has over time increased their level of commitment to the organization in a diversity of critical ways.

Second, I continue to see the value of including people in the creation process – particularly those you want involved in what you're building. The most vivid example – outside of the Sustainable Waterloo volunteer team – is a working group we struck just before launching our first initiative in the spring of 2009. We were challenged with the need to create a framework for how future members of our Regional Carbon Initiative would commit to reducing their greenhouse gas (GHG) emissions. There were many ways to set it up, many decisions to make, and many approaches to the problem. So, we did the research required to come up with a variety of options, we created a decision tree for these options, and we solicited participation in this working group from those organizations we hoped would be future members.

This working group met over the course of 4 months, and truthfully, they made some decisions that I likely wouldn't have made. But by giving them control – while armed with the information required to make wise decisions – they developed a sense of ownership in the outcome of the process. To-date, 86% of the 22 original working group members are now clients, Board members, or event sponsors of Sustainable Waterloo. These are the people who later got us meetings with their own management teams, championed Sustainable Waterloo in their organizations, and ultimately became our most dedicated supporters.

Third, the reality is that transformative ideas affect more than one sector - more than one subset of a community. We found it was critical to bring these diverse organizations together with a common goal in mind: to make tangible progress toward a low-carbon economy. By working toward this common goal, organizations were able to collaborate and learn from each other without the competitive tension inherent in many business relationships.

For example, Sustainable Waterloo routinely hosts events where accountants are sitting across from engineers, sustainability professionals, and academics. Every discipline has its own unique perspective, knowledge-base and challenges when it comes to reducing GHG emissions. This creates dynamic interactions when discussing their common ground: they all work in buildings of similar constructions, they all need to figure out how to transport employees to and from work, and they all report to decision-makers focused on profit. When brought together, they are able to support one another, and as a result, make quicker and more efficient progress towards their own GHG reductions.

Fourth, I am very supportive of having a model to point to that demonstrates at least a core element of the idea being championed. In our case, my co-founder and I were lucky to draw inspiration, mentorship, and credibility for Sustainable Waterloo from a similar organization that had been operating for several years in Silicon Valley. Although we needed to shape the model in many ways for the political, cultural, and institutional realities of our community, the core idea was already market-tested. This existing model first led us to believe in the possibility of a similar organization in Waterloo Region. Not only that, our San Francisco-based mentors shared lessons learned that allowed us to move more quickly than ever without them. And their successes allowed us to point out to funders, grantors, and our first clients, an example of how our proposed model works. In short, the Silicon Valley model brought to life our ideas and plans for our stakeholders.

Last, whenever I meet someone who expresses interest in supporting the work of Sustainable Waterloo – be it at a conference, job fair, or on the street – I always give them a menu of options to do so, and I follow-up as quickly as I can. This combination of follow-through and self-selection has been critical, and is now a practice of the organization. The premise is simple: everyone in Waterloo Region has a role to play in what we're building. So, our task is simply to help identify that role and figure out how an individual's support is mutually beneficial for them and for Sustainable Waterloo. This means I rarely go places looking simply to find a potential new client, or to just uncover a new funding opportunity. It means I go places to meet people, to share our vision with them, and to see if they want to be a part of it, whatever that means to them. It could be just in terms of staying informed of our work, or in participating in a working group, on the Board, or volunteering.

For example, when we were getting Sustainable Waterloo off the ground, I was lucky enough to meet a particularly influential leader from the Waterloo business community. He was interested in our work and wanted to support us. I assumed this individual would either provide funding or connect us with his previous employer, a large tech firm in Waterloo Region. But after I explained the various ways he could help, he realized his greatest contribution would be to share his extensive experience and help guide the organization's direction as a Board member. Sustainable Waterloo has benefited immensely from his insights ever since. I have come to realize that my job is to get people excited about what we want to accomplish, and allow potential supporters to tell us how they would like help accomplish it.

It's these 5 practices that have brought Sustainable Waterloo from an idea to what I'd consider a successful venture. Without them, I'm positive we wouldn't have the level of stakeholder buy in that we do. Our people are invested in our success, and we're invested in theirs. It's sincere. It's win-win. And I've found it's a successful model for the adoption of any new idea you want people to champion.

Key takeaways:

- Focus on building long-standing relationships
- Be sure to include people in the process of change
- Harness different perspectives by collaborating across all sectors
- Try to leverage existing models, while taking risks to adapt as needed
- Always provide supporters with a menu of options to contribute

Mike Morrice

Mike is the co-founder and Executive Director of Sustainable Waterloo, a not-for-profit that advances the environmental sustainability of organizations across Waterloo Region through collaboration.

Currently, Sustainable Waterloo works with dozens of local organizations – including Wilfrid Laurier University, Sun Life Financial, and the Region of Waterloo – to help them set and make progress against voluntary carbon reduction commitments. More information is available online at www.sustainablewaterloo.org.

Mike is a 2008 graduate of Wilfrid Laurier University, where he concurrently completed a BBA and a BSc in Computing and Computer Electronics. In 2009, Mike was selected by The Waterloo Region Record as one of Waterloo Region's Top 40 under 40.

Lessons Learned Along the Way:
You have to Care

Ted Hastings

It was just another interview for an opportunity that appeared interesting on the surface – Vice President Finance of a spinoff from The Descartes Systems Group. I made my way over to Mark Lee's house to meet him for the first time with my resume in hand. I was twenty-five years old with freshly minted CA and CPA designations under my belt from my position at Deloitte & Touche in Kitchener.

It was early 2000 and the stock market was soaring.

I knew very little of Mark other than he was an early investor in Descartes and had retired from active duty when Descartes went public on the Toronto Stock Exchange.

The interview was several hours. The questions ranged from my personal life, business experience (or lack thereof) and with each question he tossed up I attacked it with textbook-rich responses.

He wrapped up that first session with what seemed to be a gimme but he asked it with such intensity that I knew that no matter what my answer involved, it was going to fall short.

"Ok Teddy. This is an important one. What do you think it takes to have a successful business?"

That's it? That's the big question? What do you think it takes to have a successful business?

"That's easy Mark. Hard work, strong leadership, a good market opportunity, product vision and execution, sales, marketing…" and I carried on in that vein for several more minutes before Mark gracefully cut me off.

"Teddy, that's all well and good but I want you to listen closely to me on this one. Everything you said makes sense and they are all ingredients to a successful business but there is one thing I want you to remember throughout your career and especially if we are going to be partners in this new venture. If you want to have the opportunity to be associated with successful businesses throughout your career – you have to care. It's that simple. You have to care. Each and every day you wake up you have to care about your coworkers, your customers, the products you put in the market, your suppliers, partners and investors. You have to care. So many people go through the motions to get through their days. So many people are busy and hardworking but lack true passion for what they are working towards. If you care, if you really care... you have a shot at being successful."

Throughout my career – through the opportunities and the challenges – I have never forgotten the contagious experience of sitting across the table from someone who was truly passionate about his business and who made something so complicated seem so obviously simple.

To have a successful business you have to care. Simple.

Hire an All-star

I had just turned twenty-six and found myself in the position of CEO of a software company that later became known as GBG.

With absolute certainty I knew one thing – I had no idea what I was doing.

Sales, marketing, operations, HR, product development, finance. Perhaps I could check the finance box and that was it. Even that may have even been a stretch, I knew how to audit.

We had customers, products, employees and a CEO who was basically a recent university graduate.

I knew I was outgunned, so I did the only thing that made sense. I retained and hired some gunslingers to help me out.

It is impossible to properly describe the experience of working alongside a team of all-stars to someone who has never made that investment. It is the equivalent of telling expectant parents that their lives are going to change forever knowing that it is only after they welcome the baby that they are then able to look you in the eye and give you that understanding smile.

I have avoided some of the pitfalls that often surround a founder who has enjoyed some level of success early in his or her career. That success can sometimes breed an unwillingness to change the complexion of their executive team or cloud the need to find a successor CEO. I needed help and hired the best talent I could attract and paid them as much as I could afford and then some.

All-stars never disappoint with their work ethic. They are workaholics who have learned to harness their addiction. They will surprise you with their creativity and surround you with their loyalty when the team is challenged. You never have to guess what they are doing on a Saturday night.

An all-star believes the impossible remains possible at even the darkest moments in the life of a company.

That clarity of vision associated with my situation at that time has been a tremendous asset for me throughout my career. I hired all-stars to fill out my executive team. They understood my passion and educated me on their areas of expertise.

Our team took a business that was losing money, customers and employees and over the following five years we acquired nine competitors, added 150 employees and became the market leaders in our industry.

We sold the company to 3M November 1st, 2006 and threw a party fit for a team of all-stars.

The Great Collapse

There are moments in your career that no amount of success can mask.

I was hired on as President of Geosign in January of 2007. In March of that same year we raised US $160 million in Canada's largest private equity financing in several years and weeks later our revenues dropped, overnight, to nearly zero.

Similar to watching a champion racehorse experience a career ending injury midrace, we were stunned.

Geosign was an internet company that relied entirely on Google for our customers and Google terminated our business model – in a matter of minutes.

What do you do when your business crumbles to the ground? What do you do when your real time graph of your traffic/customers nosedives until it settles on the X-axis?

There are times in your personal and professional life when you are faced with nearly impossible odds. At those times you have a simple choice:

You can quit.

You can stay and fight.

In the intense silence of that evening I had a few minutes to think over my choices and settled on the only one that seemed fitting of the amazing challenge ahead. It was time to put our backs against the wall and fight until we either built the business back or admitted defeat in what would go down as one of the greatest collapses in recent Canadian business history.

I started by drawing on the basic fundamentals that I had leaned on in my career to that point – you have to care and I needed to retain the all-stars I had on staff as well as attract some new ones to the fire.

We drafted a new business plan.

We renegotiated with our investors.

We charted the shortest path we could between the current state of financial affairs and breakeven.

We invested in talent and new business lines.

We turned to our business partners and requested help.

We started to execute against our plan with a daily checkpoint and put some numbers, slowly, back on the board.

We bought the assets of Geosign in September 2007 and formed Moxy Media. The following twelve months were a continuation of our rebuilding efforts until we started to hit our stride in 2009.

In 2009 we grew our revenues by over $100 million reclaiming our post as one of Canada's largest internet companies.

The Geosign experiment proved my hypothesis that a team of passionate all-stars that care... can move mountains.

Perspective

I have spent a good amount of time during my career on the road – visiting customers, prospects, remote offices, investors, acquisition targets and potential partners. It is a necessary evil if you are going to build a business. The work/life balance is something I have yet to master.

In mid 2008 I had an idea that I would write a daily letter to my two children. The letters would be about my days – the challenges and opportunities, successes and failures. In addition they would document the little things that my children had done that day. The things you forget years down the road and that they never had a chance to remember in the first place given their age.

I bought their domain names and simply linked it to a wordpress account and I was off to the races.

After a few weeks of a post here and a post there it became a daily event without fail. My obsessive tendencies were on display for my children to witness through these letters.

It is an avenue for me to connect daily with my family even on days when I am far from their bedside as is often the case as you build a business.

It gives me some peace of mind to know that while I am out slaying dragons there has never been a day where I didn't stop and tell them about their daddy and what they mean to me.

It allows me to keep all of the intensity that is involved with working alongside entrepreneurs in check.

It gives me perspective... daily.

Summary

My career has ranged from developing software for a complex distribution environment, a rollup of a cottage industry and participating in one of the more dynamic markets in existence today – the online advertising game. Regardless of the unique aspects of the industries in which I have competed, I have relied on a core set of fundamental principles that have allowed me to survive some close calls and to take advantage of opportunities as they have presented themselves:

To have a successful business **you need to care** – each and every day you wake up you have to care about your coworkers, your customers, the products you put in the market, your suppliers, partners and investors

Seek out, attract and retain all-stars. They will manage through the seemingly impossible situations with calm and confidence. Their passion will elevate your game and their unwavering loyalty will give you peace of mind to lead your organization.

Compete – especially when everyone has already counted you out. Those victories make for great career stories.

Do something to **maintain your perspective**, daily. You never know when your business might collapse overnight and at that moment –a healthy perspective might be all that you have on your side.

Ted Hastings

Ted Hastings has more than ten years of corporate experience in a variety of industries. As a founder and operator of both small private and large technology businesses, Ted has leadership experience and unique insight from how to grow businesses to multiple exits, including a major disposition to a F100 public company.

Ted currently serves as President and Chief Executive Officer at Moxy Media. Prior to that, he served as President at Geosign, where he was instrumental in completing a US $160 million private equity financing.

Before his work at Geosign, Ted was responsible for the post-acquisition integration of Global Beverage Group (GBG) with High Jump Software, a division of 3M. As Chief Executive Officer of GBG for five years, Ted increased the company's value through a series of nine acquisitions, ultimately culminating in the sale of GBG to 3M, a Fortune 100 Company.

Ted holds a Bachelor of Business Administration from Wilfrid Laurier University and earned his CA and CPA designations during his four years at Deloitte & Touche LLP.

Time Management

Adam Zimmer

In running a start-up, entrepreneurs are always conscious of maximizing utilization of scarce resources. Certainly every entrepreneur is used to maximizing available working capital. However, many are not necessarily aware of an even scarcer resource: their time. Time is, of course, a finite quantity and fundamentally cannot be replaced. In particular the time of the management team is incredibly expensive. While an entrepreneur may not realize the value of his or her time, they are often the firm's most valuable employee.

To look at it another way, assume a firm is trying to raise working capital, an entrepreneur would have several options:

a) increase revenue – this could be accomplished by more marketing, sales or even product management to ensure the product is filling a market need

b) raise capital – the entrepreneur could look at bringing in outside investors or even at later stages an IPO

However, if an entrepreneur misallocates his/her time everything suffers including revenue and consequently makes raising capital more difficult.

Below I have attempted to share some of the ways I have found to maximize the utilization of my time.

Prioritization

This sounds very easy but is in effect one of the most difficult strategies to implement. At its simplest it involves analyzing what tasks need to be completed and the importance of each. The challenge of course is determining the importance of each. Sometimes this is obvious, for example, dealing with an important customer issue in a timely manner. However, in many cases it is much less clear cut and the probabilities of success must be weighed against the benefits and time commitment eg. Developing partnerships that may lead to greater revenue down the road but require substantial investments of time in developing interest from the partner, negotiating contracts etc..

In addition, it comes as a shock to many entrepreneurs that they will never complete all their low priority tasks. This brings to mind a story about the implementation of one of the first mainframes. On the day it was installed a low priority task was created. Years later when it was decommissioned it was observed that the task never ran.

One approach many entrepreneurs take to the detriment of their work/life balance and family life is to simply do more. However, I have found that this is a dangerous approach for the business. In many cases doing the right things is more important than just keeping busy. Determining the right things takes a clarity of vision which is difficult to achieve when you are stuck in the trenches. I have found that my best insights come when my utilization is no greater than 90%. The last 10% allows me to discover what I have been missing. These items could be the result of misprioritization or were not even on the list until I was able to synthesize what my employees, customers and investors were telling me.

As an entrepreneur there is always another thing that you could be doing. The corollary to this: is it a task you *should* be doing?

Delegation

This is something that differentiates consultants from managers. Over the years I have been privileged to work with many talented individuals however, only some of them could manage. As an entrepreneur I have seen two types of other entrepreneurs: those who could manage, and those who couldn't. In many cases some of the more talented individuals I met were great at doing things well but their businesses were fundamentally limited by their ability to allow others to help them.

The excuses were fairly typical: their employees didn't do as good a job as they did, they couldn't count on their employees to take ownership, the project was running late and their employees had gone home, etc... In general though I found these to be indicative of other problems.

Quality – Quality control is something that is very important in a start-up. Your competitors in most cases are much larger (and often slower) but tend to have established track records. As a start-up you have to build a track record and quality issues can quickly erode good will. While no entrepreneur is perfect, in general they will go the extra mile to ensure the quality of the work they do. When they delegate a task this is difficult to pass along. Consequently, I have found that having a good quality control process allows for delegation. In some cases this could be reviewing the materials prepared by others, in other cases it could be a good automated test suite.

Ownership – When I first started my business I felt it was my duty to ensure that my employees were given an environment where they could succeed. I naively assumed that this was an environment free from distractions in which they could focus on doing the best work possible. This created an awkward scenario where customers had demands which they expressed to me, and I in turn would relay them to developers. In many cases I felt like a trailer hitch as all the stress and strain of reconciling the two groups fell on me. As our business grew and I was forced to delegate I realized that I had to pass through all of this information to my mid-level managers who in turn could pass this along to the developers. That way each of them knew why they were doing what they were doing and were able to understand the actions of management.

Overloading – This is one of the areas that I have found gives people the most difficulty. They assume that their employees are very busy. In fact they likely are but they are being robbed of the opportunity to maximize their time if you try to do it for them. I have found that giving employees visibility into deadlines and customer requirements allows them to better schedule their time and also the time of their developers. In the end there will always be exceptional cases where management intervention is needed but with good planning these will be fewer and farther between; a heavy load is lighter when spread over many people.

Estimation – To manage effectively I have found that accurately estimating the effort involved in tasks is important, however even creating inaccurate estimates is infinitely better than having none at all. Estimates allow for gating of tasks; if a task exceeds the estimate, manager involvement may be necessary. Alternatively, if an estimate appears unreasonable before a task has even begun perhaps an alternate approach is required.

Out-sourcing

Out-sourcing is something usually associated with large companies and foreign locations with cheaper labour costs. Certainly not something most associate with start-ups. However, in many cases a more limited version of outsourcing can yield significant time savings.

A key criteria in developing an outsourcing strategy is determining your firm's core competency. This is the one thing that your firm does really well (hopefully). This is what you don't want to outsource. Everything else should be examined.

In the world of software, this allowed our business to save significant resources. In particular at one point we were looking at adding some document recognition capabilities into our software. We quickly discovered that the cost of not just developing but maintaining this software far exceeded the cost of using a third party library. This saved not only development, support and manager time but also allowed us to focus our product management on differentiating our product in our core competencies and not trying to re-invent the wheel.

Other areas to examine are Software As A Service. Maintaining and supporting infrastructure is expensive and time consuming. Many start-ups have benefited from the low incremental cost of utilizing shared infrastructure for CRM, E-mail and other systems.

However, one important caveat is to watch the technology adoption curve. Geoffrey Moore has made famous his crossing the chasm model of technology adoption. One trap many entrepreneurs fall into is becoming technology enthusiasts and adopting technology too early. I purchased an iPhone as soon as it was offered in Canada. Six months later I decided I could not afford to keep using it. The reason was simple – it was costing me time. No software existed to turn it off at night and on in the morning. This wasted precious minutes a day and occasionally resulted in a 3 am wake-up e-mail when I forgot to turn on the mute mode. In general, I have found that the early majority is where you want to be. Early enough to be ahead of your competition but not so early that you need to be helping your supplier perfect their product.

Technology to Extend your Presence

You can't be in two places at once. Nor can you attend two meetings at once, however with a little inconvenience and some technology, you can come close.

Meeting in person is always preferable for any number of reasons from reading body language, to developing a personal connection in the few minutes before the meeting. However web conferencing tools have allowed me to have more meetings than I ever could have if I had to fly to each customer.

Similarly, phone forwarding has allowed me to get unscheduled customer calls at 6:30 am without having to be in the office. This has allowed me to go places and do things that would have been impossible several years ago.

In addition, remote desktop access allows employees to work from home in cases of inclement weather but also allows you to check that a long running program completed successfully at 9 pm at night.

These technologies collectively can allow you to utilize your time more efficiently from avoiding travel time to having to be at the office late in case someone calls. Unfortunately while these technologies offer a temporary advantage they quickly become a necessity since even if you don't use them you can count on the fact that your competitors will.

Summary

In summary, you are the heart of your business. No matter what, the one thing you control is your time. By utilizing it well through prioritization, delegation, outsourcing and extending your presence you can multiply your effectiveness.

Adam Zimmer

Adam is President and CEO of Arius Software, has over 10 years experience in the software industry. In 1999, seeing a deluge of new opportunities for dynamic programming on the Internet, he launched Arius Software Corporation. While at NCR, Adam won second place in a programming competition for creating a web-enabled banking solution. This experience provided the needed insight for Arius to win its first enterprise-wide solution in the Financial Services market. Currently, Adam supplies the long-term vision and financial management for the company.

Strategizing for Maximum Value

William M. Tatham

After selling my first company in a record value transaction in 2000, people told me I was lucky – and I was. In fact, I'd like to be lucky again, but I also believe that luck on its own is not enough to succeed in business. Like Thomas Jefferson once said, "I'm a great believer in luck, and I find the harder I work, the more I have of it." Indeed, our timing was lucky. The stars aligned and the capital markets peaked, and we sold near the top of the NASDAQ technology bubble in 2000. The fact that we were able to sell our business at a premium, however, wasn't luck, but the culmination of our *strategy to maximize value*.

The first thing I would say about entrepreneurial endeavours – and it defines the business strategy we employ at my current company, NexJ Systems, and any other entrepreneurial endeavour that I'm involved in – is strategize for maximum value. That's it. I'm not interested in being number one at something in Toronto. I'm not interested in being the biggest thing in Canada. It's got to be global. We've got to be the best in the world at what we do, because that's what pays the most. If a strategy does not maximize our leverage and the value that we get out of our investment of time, effort, and money that we put in, then we do not follow that strategy. I don't understand entrepreneurs who would follow a business strategy without understanding how they can get the maximum value out of their efforts.

Learn From Others

Do you really want to be an entrepreneur? In my experience, the school of hard knocks is a painful teacher, so the best advice I can give you is to learn on somebody else's nickel first. It's best to work in a successful company and understand as much as you can about that company – and how to run it, manage it, and operate it – before you try and do it yourself.

Continuous commitment to learning, self-improvement, and self-actualization is important. The more you know, the greater success you are likely to have. Even now, after more than 20 years of business experience and three successful ventures, I am still learning. For example, I currently serve on the board of directors at Elizabeth Arden, a global fragrance and prestige beauty products company, where I sit on the Audit and Compensation Committees. NexJ Systems, the company

I currently run, provides enterprise CRM software for the financial services, insurance, and healthcare industries. So, if I run a software company, why am I on the board of a fragrance and beauty company? What's in it for NexJ? For me, this is my extended MBA. It's a great place for me to study modern corporate governance directly and get exposure to running a much larger company than NexJ is today.

The rapid growth at my first company, Janna Systems, a leading provider of CRM software to Wall Street firms, taught me the importance of studying larger, more successful firms. At the time I said "You know, I'm not really qualified to run a company this big, because it's twice the size of any company I've ever run before". Janna was doubling in size every year and I realized that if we were going to succeed, it was important for me to get out in front and learn more about how to govern a larger organization.

Model for Success – The Janna Systems Story

After graduating from the University of Waterloo, I spent seven years working at a handful of successful companies before I left and founded Janna in my basement. Janna Systems' initial focus was on retail contact management software. Each year, as our product got better and better, the price dropped lower and lower, until the final version was the best and cheapest we had ever produced. We were selling our product for only $49 per package, and 40-60% of our selling price was spent on retail distribution.

Ultimately, we had a near death experience with retail software, which we managed to avoid because we continuously ran a quantitative business model (quant model). Quant models enable you to work out the details behind your business: your starting cash, your plan for a worst case revenue scenario, and your monthly spend. At one point, our quant model showed us that our *monthly* revenue run rate was equal to our *weekly* promotion cost requirements. That's when we knew it was time to move beyond retail software. We decided to grow our business in a new direction by looking at precedent business models and determining what would work for us.

After careful analysis, we decided to move to a direct enterprise software business model. We re-architected our product for enterprise deployment and developed deep domain expertise in a narrow vertical market: financial services or, more specifically, institutional brokerage and investment banking. By focusing on a narrow go-to-market strategy, we were able to develop in-depth vertical market expertise that enabled us to provide an extremely high level of customer service. We continually improved the product based on customer feedback and broader enterprise requirements, and our service division adapted our solution to meet our customers' unique business needs. This approach gave our customers a more innovative, tailored offering, and allowed us to generate revenue from providing additional support services.

Selling critical software to large corporations directly meant that we could greatly increase our average transaction size. We believe average transaction size is the single greatest determinant of gross margin. If you're selling cars, for example, you have a potential to make more profit selling a Rolls Royce than a Volkswagen. At Janna, increasing our transaction size meant that instead of selling two to three units at $49 each and losing a large amount of the selling price through the distribution channel, we sold directly to the companies, selling 1000 units at $1000 each, and we were able to pocket more of the selling price.

Once Janna moved to a direct enterprise sales model, we were able to grow the company rapidly, increasing quarterly revenue for 16 consecutive quarters until our acquisition in late 2000. Our clients consisted of the leading names in financial services, including Goldman Sachs, Merril Lynch, Morgan Stanley, JP Morgan, and others. Eventually, we sold Janna to our largest competitor, Siebel Systems, for $1.76 billion in 2000.

Analyze What Works

After selling Janna, the management team received numerous calls from companies who asked us to sit on their boards, and from venture capitalists who asked us for advice on how to improve the performance of their investee companies. Given the demand for our advisory services, in 2002 we founded XJ Partners, a venture capital and advisory services firm focused on early stage technology companies.

At XJ Partners, we chose to invest in what we knew – enterprise software. Investing in early stage technology companies is inherently "high risk"; however, by investing in what we knew, we felt that we could better manage that risk. We sought out companies with innovative technology and invested in those companies if they followed a proven business model. While there are no guarantees in business, we had a firm belief that if you strategize for maximum value, work hard, and execute with an immediacy of action, your chances of success are greatly improved.

Confident in our success at Janna, and wanting to recreate this success with our investee firms, we distilled our success down to a few key points that we believe work for software companies:

Enterprise Software – You can maximize your transaction size by focusing on enterprise software.

Direct Sales Model – You can increase your success by adopting a direct sales model and taking charge of your own distribution. We learned that from a marketing perspective, it is cheaper and easier to sell directly to customers than to create consumer demand through an indirect distribution channel.

Extreme Market Focus—You can greatly benefit from focusing on being the very best in a narrowly defined market. Having a defined market focus enabled us to compete with companies 50 times our size at Janna Systems. Niche boutiques can deliver higher service levels than broad market suppliers, and at both Janna and NexJ our focus has allowed us to function as a strategic partner to our customers.

Compelling Technology – Differentiating the company based on the strength of the technology and the rate of innovation is key to being successful. The software industry is a hamster wheel, and you should never stop spinning and improving your product. In our opinion, when evaluating the success of a technology company, the rate of technical evolution is more important than the uniqueness of the technology.

Commitment to Customer Service Level – It is important to commit to providing exemplary customer service. In enterprise software, the customer's level of satisfaction with your products and services is paramount. At NexJ, we follow what I like to call a *self-correcting, revenue-seeking, product management model*. There are two parts to this model: 1) give customers exactly what they want (our narrow market focus helps with that); 2) charge them for it. A company should take customer feedback and requirements and build these into the product – at a reasonable price. This is a win-win situation. Customers receive what they want; and you make money while you evolve and improve your software at the same time.

Develop the Right Strategy, Tactics, and Culture for Success

From our experience at XJ Partners, we knew that applying the right business strategy isn't enough. How you execute your strategy is just as important. As a result, we devised three determinants of success for maximizing value, which we describe using the analogy of firing a gun:

1. *Aim the Weapon (Strategy)* – What you work on should be in-line with the target you are trying to hit. What is your strategy? Which customer pain points are you trying to address? What is your target market? Who are your competitors? If everything you're working on comes to fruition, where do you end up? Are you where you want to be? If not, you need to reconsider your aim.

2. *Pull the Trigger (Tactics)* – No matter how good the strategy, you still have to pull the trigger – that's tactics and operations. You have to understand all of the processes required to measure, manage, and control

the daily operations of your company. Hopefully you don't waver and you hit the target. The success of your business strategy is dependent on the accuracy of your operational execution.

3. *If You Miss the Target (Culture)* – What are you going to do if you miss the target? How quickly do you pull the trigger again? How many times? Will you re-aim first? In my experience this is a question of corporate culture. Firms need to execute with a greater sense of urgency. At XJ Partners, we had reasonable success, but many of our investee companies could have been much more successful if they had executed with a sense of urgency. *Now* is the time for positive action.

Strategize for Maximum Value: 3 Levels of Value

Another lesson we learned from our experience at Janna Systems and XJ Partners is that you must understand what determines value before you can maximize it. In our opinion, there are three levels that determine value:

3 Levels of Value

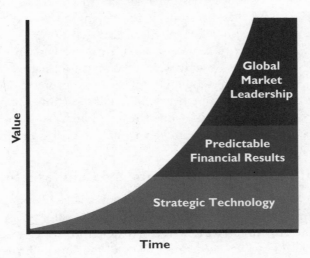

Figure 5– Three Levels of Business Value

Strategic Technology – Strategic technology is technology so cool it may change or save the world. People will want to buy the company just to get their hands on this technology.

Predictable Financial Results – If you can sell the technology into the market so that you generate a predictable and projectable revenue stream, then that company should be of higher value – this is called the commercialization stage.

Global Market Leadership – If all that revenue comes from a relevant and defined market segment or niche, such that you have a legitimate claim on *global market leadership*, then that's by far and away the highest level of value that you can get. If you are number one in the world at what you do, then you should be worth more than any of your competitors.

We like to define a relevant target market as one that has a $1 billion dollar annual recurring spend. Choosing a large, relevant market will give your company enough market head room to grow. We also believe that it is important to set goals for measuring your success. For a start-up company, we generally set goal of $100 million in revenue. This is an ambitious goal, but we like to set a high bar for success. However, in a market that has over $1 billion in annual recurring spend you should be able to achieve a $100 million revenue run rate.

Strategic market selection is another important concept, as it drives strategic market position. We strongly recommend reading Geoffrey Moore's books "Crossing the Chasm" and "Inside the Tornado", which were excellent resources for us when we were developing our go-to-market strategy. In these books, Moore rationalizes the process of expansion into other, related markets. With any start up, you generally sell one product (Product 1) into one market (Market 1). Then, you can accelerate your growth by selling that same product into a new market (Market 2), or by selling a slightly different product (Product 2) into the same market (Market 1).

Selling Product 1 into Market 1, however, should be sufficient to succeed. You don't want your success to be dependent on entering subsequent markets. Expanding into different markets or products can create strategic inflection points that can lead to corporate failure. By initially focusing on a relevant market, you have enough room to grow your company without relying on entering subsequent markets.

What determines the value of your Company?

Aside from the three levels of business value, stock price is another measure of value. From our experience, we believe that stock price is a function of three things:

$$\text{Stock Price} \sim f\left\{\begin{array}{c}\text{Strategic} \\ \text{Market} \\ \text{Position}\end{array}, \text{CAGR}, \text{Earnings}\right\}$$

Strategic Market Position – The strategic market position refers to your company's relative standing in the comparable universe of all companies that compete in your sector. The stronger your position in your target market, the higher multiple capital markets will assign to you (i.e., multiple to sales or earnings). This is why I preach the idea of global market leadership. Not only is it the strongest competitive position in a market, but it is also the position most highly valued by capital markets, as evidenced by the last page in any investment analyst report, which compares your company against other companies that compete in the same sector.

Compound Annual Growth Rate – The compound annual growth rate (CAGR) represents the year-over-year growth rate at which a company is growing. At NexJ, we plan to double each year. It is an ambitious goal, but we believe that those who don't plan for it, rarely achieve it! The faster you are growing, the faster your value as a company increases, because capital markets tend to put a premium on higher growth companies.

Earnings – While we believe that revenue growth and a break-even level of profitability is more important for smaller, younger companies, for moderate or slow growth companies, maximizing earnings is the key to maximizing company valuations. Technology companies that are looking to maximize CAGR, however, fix earnings as part of their strategic market position. At Janna Systems, knowing our minimum expected revenue against planned expenses enabled us to know exactly how much cash we would have at end of year. At our current stage of growth, we'd be happy with 1¢ per share annual earnings, just to prove that we can be profitable. We would seek to invest all other revenues into driving growth for the company.

In our opinion, start-ups should *always* maintain a 12-month supply of cash; otherwise, insolvency threatens. Cash on hand means life or death for your company, so if you don't have this saved up, don't wait, raise this money!

Why Go Public?

Going public, such as listing the company's shares on an exchange like the TSX through an IPO, can be a challenging but rewarding process. On the downside, being public opens the company up to constant scrutiny and a requirement to perform almost flawlessly every quarter (or risk seeing the stock price collapse). However, on the upside, publicly traded companies often enjoy a higher valuation than private companies and they provide shareholders with liquidity.

To value a company, investors like to use various techniques: such as a price/earnings ratio or a price to sales multiple. As a private company, your company is typically valued based on a multiple of your previous year's revenue. This is what is referred to as *trailing revenue multiple valuation.* As a public company, your stock price is usually based on a forward-looking or *prospective revenue multiple valuation* of the company where you are valued based on analyst estimates of how the company will do next year. Switching from a trailing valuation to a prospective valuation, at 100% CAGR, using the same revenue multiple, means your company is worth twice the value.

Strong revenue multiple valuations are dependent on sustaining high CAGR. Having exceptionally good forward visibility in your business is very important and predictability should therefore be a key component in the decision to go public. If the company does not meet expectations once you go public, clawing your way back to credibility from a missed quarter can be an exceptionally long and painful process.

Exit Strategy

The Janna Systems sale highlights that to exit at the highest value possible, dominating a relevant market niche, maximizing CAGR, and running a profitable operating model leads to the highest valuation.

How did we manage to sell Janna to our largest competitor for 100% control premium? We went back to our concept that stock price is a function of strategic market position, compound annual growth rate, and earnings.

Strategic Market Position – At Janna, we bested our largest competitor 8 out of 8 times in multi-million dollar deals over our last two years. As a result, we had a legitimate claim to being the global market leader in our target market. This market was strategic for our competition, which significantly increased the value of our company.

CAGR – At Janna we could show that we had reliably doubled the size of the company for the last six years and that we were on track for doing it again. As such, if market conditions held constant, we could reasonably expect our stock price to double again in the next 12 months.

Earnings – Janna was highly profitable and we had achieved self-sustaining, organic growth. We didn't *need* more money, and we didn't need to sell the company.

These factors put us in a position of power in negotiations. Since we reasonably expected our stock price to double in the next 12 months and were confident in our market position, we saw no reason to sell at anything less than an advance of one year's growth or 100% control premium, which suggested two times the current stock price. If you sell your company at 100% control premium (see Figure 6) you get another double!

Time Frame	Revenue	3x Revenue Multiple		
		Private	Public	Exit
Last Year	$50,000,000			
This Year	$100,000,000	3x Last Year	3x This Year	3x Next Year
		$150,000,000	$300,000,000	$600,000,000

Figure 6– Example of Current Company Value at 3x Revenue Multiple When Private, Public, and Exiting if Consistently Growing at 100% CAGR *For illustrative purposes only.*

Give Back

Now that I've started a new venture, the most frequent question I get is "Why did you do this again?"

One reason was to prove that our success at Janna wasn't just luck. Our strategies work. We were able to test them at XJ Partners, but too many companies failed to execute with an immediacy of action and did not prosper as much as we knew they could have.

Another reason was our passion to win. We saw an opening in the market, we knew our strategies worked, and we could make significant equity returns, so why not? We'd have been foolish to overlook this opportunity.

In the end, however, these reasons were not enough. What really motivated us to do it all again was our desire to give back to society, particularly in the area of healthcare. Healthcare had a personal connection for me. Shortly after Janna was acquired, my family suffered a health crisis. During this time, I realized that many of the pressing issues facing healthcare – maintaining the quality of care, ensuring patient safety, and managing the cost and scope of services – could be solved by applying a people-centered model. People-centered healthcare would enable patients to access a comprehensive shared electronic health record for all patients and allow care providers to collaborate across the continuum of care.

We knew we could bring our innovative technology to enable change in the world of healthcare. This, ultimately, was our goal when we founded NexJ Systems – bringing about a fundamental shift to people-centered healthcare. This is not a small goal, and it will take time to achieve, but we firmly believe that if we use what we've learned from others, apply our proven business strategy, and execute with a sense of urgency, we can repeat our previous success in healthcare. This time, however, we seek not only to maximize the value of our company, but to make a meaningful and substantive contribution to society.

William M. Tatham

William M. Tatham is the Chief Executive Officer of NexJ Systems Inc., a premier provider of people-centric enterprise business solutions for the financial services, insurance, and healthcare industries.

Prior to establishing NexJ Systems in 2003, Mr. Tatham was the Founder, Chairman and CEO of Janna Systems, which he sold to his largest competitor, Siebel Systems, in a $1.76 billion record value transaction for a Canadian software company. He was also a partner at XJ Partners, a company of strategic investors in software technology which he founded in 2002 along with the former management of Janna Systems Inc.

Mr. Tatham is a member of the Board of Elizabeth Arden (RDEN: NASQ), a global prestige beauty, fragrance, cosmetics and skincare products company where he sits on the Audit and Compensation committees. He is actively involved in health and education and a former member of the Board of Governors at the University of Waterloo.

Mr. Tatham is a graduate from the University of Waterloo in 1983, with a Bachelor of Applied Science in Systems Design Engineering and options in Socio-economic Systems and Management Science.

It's All About the Value Proposition

Ray DePaul

I'm sitting at a table at the crowded Duke of Wellington in Uptown Waterloo finishing off my second Guinness, when a polite university student approaches and asks whether I'm almost done with the table. Sensing I had a captive audience for a few minutes, I decide to impart some wisdom on the young lad before giving up my table and the half-eaten chips and curry. I decide today's lecture would be about value propositions, the need to focus and pivot, and the art of looking bigger than you are. The poor chap never knew what hit him.

The Value Proposition

Much has been written about the need for a powerful value proposition, yet I continue to be surprised at how few entrepreneurs invest the energy and discipline in truly understanding their unique value proposition. Customers, partners and investors will all judge you by your value proposition. Nail this and doors and ears will be opened.

I wish I had devised something truly unique in this area, but I haven't found any reason to innovate beyond what Geoffrey Moore has been espousing for a couple of decades around what he calls a *positioning statement*. Grab a couple of colleagues, lock yourself in a windowless room for a few hours and apply the following template to your idea, technology, or product.

For (target customer or market)

Who (have a specific problem or a compelling reason to buy)

Our product is a (new/existing product category)

That provides (key benefit that directly addresses the compelling reason to buy)

Unlike (the reference competitor/alternative)

Our product (provides a meaningful differentiator for the target customer).

When performing this exercise, it's important to understand that you're not writing copy for your website. You are defining important elements of your product and business that will drive sales, marketing, and product development. Everyone in the company should understand and believe in the value proposition.

The original BlackBerry value proposition went something like this:

For mobile business users,

Who want to stay on top of their email,
BlackBerry is a wireless handheld
That provides access to corporate email anytime, anywhere.
Unlike a laptop with a modem,
BlackBerry pushes corporate email to you in real-time.

In devising this value proposition, there were a few key decisions that I believe contributed to BlackBerry's early success. The first is RIM's famous focus on the business segment, which demanded that the product have enterprise-class security, an earlier differentiator that continues to serve RIM well. But as importantly, it was the *mobile* user in business. If you spent most of your workday behind your desk, you were not in the target market. Of course, there were many BlackBerry users that fit this profile, but we ensured that the product and limited sales and marketing resources were aimed at the professional who spent a good deal of time out of the office. This decision was one of the reasons behind RIM's obsession with battery life. A user should be able to go on a weeklong trip and not have to worry about battery life. We watched as early competitors such as Microsoft ignored this requirement and failed to gain adoption.

The identification of a laptop and a modem as the primary competition is also instructive. You have to transport yourself back to the late 1990's to understand the environment BlackBerry first encountered. Early on, many observers identified RIM as being in the same category as Palm, the darling of the day with a very successful string of handhelds. But while both solutions involved a handheld device, the BlackBerry target market was not using a Palm to "stay on top of their email" – the compelling reason to buy a BlackBerry. Instead they would travel with their laptops and after a busy day on the road, would plug into the hotel data jack and download their email. This painful solution was the incumbent that BlackBerry had to displace. The compelling reason to buy a Palm, on the other hand, was to access your address book and calendar wherever you were. It turned out that it was a lot easier for RIM to encroach on Palm's value proposition than it was for Palm to add wireless email to their solution.

The early days of BlackBerry were fraught with threats. There were established brand name competitors, powerful wireless carriers, and a distracting array of opportunities. A disciplined focus on the value proposition let RIM keep everyone from management to marketing to development on the same path to dominating this new wireless handheld category.

Spend the time hashing out your value proposition. If you can concisely articulate who you are targeting, why they care, and why they should choose you, you will be closer to attracting customers or investors than most of your competition. But the process can't stop with defining your value proposition – you have to deliver on it! One of the keys to BlackBerry's success is that the solution delivers exactly on the promised value proposition. It is futile to build a company around a value proposition and then disappoint your target market with a product that doesn't meet the promise. They will not forget the underwhelming experience.

Focus… then Pivot

Focus, focus, focus. It's the mantra of most start-ups, and I couldn't agree more. But what is sometimes misunderstood is that it doesn't mean that you should stop evaluating whether you are still focusing on the right thing. A wise board member expressed it to me in this way: be 100% committed to your current strategy until the moment it is wrong. After rubbing my temples for a while, I found this advice quite freeing. I could continue to focus on one strategy, which is all I had the resources to do, but it also assumed that at some point I would determine that the strategy was wrong. Instead of ignoring the signs that I may have chosen the wrong path, I was much more in tune to what the market was telling me.

While you are focusing on executing a strategy, you are gaining valuable market insight. It only makes sense that a feedback loop as powerful as customers might cause you to change your strategy. What makes this a convergent process is that your changes to strategy will usually be a refinement rather than a completely unrelated approach. This is where the pivot metaphor comes from. With one foot firmly planted in what you are currently doing, put the other foot down on new, potentially more fertile ground. This leveraging of what you have learned by being in-market is critical and an asset new entrants don't possess.

For example, at RapidMind we made several pivots in our strategy. The lessons learned from focusing on the nascent GPU market resulted in a pivot to the more mainstream multicore CPU market. The challenges extracting licensing fees from the high performance computing industry prompted a pivot into the more receptive healthcare industry. Business development delays with one set of partners made way to a new focus on a different set of partners that ultimately resulted in the acquisition by Intel.

RIM has had several critical pivots in its history: the pivot from a hardware supplier to a solutions provider; the pivot from being a mobile virtual network operator that resold wireless airtime to supplying handhelds to hundreds of carrier partners; the pivot from business to professional consumer to consumer; the pivot from wireless email to smartphone. With the industry and competitive landscape constantly evolving, I suspect RIM has several more pivots in its future.

So, you might be wondering, when do you know it's time to pivot? Sorry, there's no magic formula, at least that I've found. All I can say is that if you stay close to customers and the market, and you are honest and reflective about the challenges you are facing, then you will be better positioned than anyone to pivot to the right destination.

The Art of Looking Big

As I shift my 5'6" frame in my seat, the irony of this topic isn't lost on me. But this is not about my stature... honest. Most entrepreneurs have an affinity for small companies, or at least working in small companies. Unfortunately not all buyers of high tech solutions share the same desire to purchase from small companies. Their fears are real and have to be addressed. Will you be around to deliver or support your product? Can you handle the demands that a growing customer base will put on your organization? Will I get fired for putting my faith in your small company? While looking bigger than you are won't eliminate all their concerns, it can go a long way in minimizing them.

One approach to heightening (pun intended) the perception of your company is to invest in public relations (PR). For about the cost of a senior headcount, you can have a boutique PR agency work on raising your profile. At RapidMind, we were successful at placing many articles authored by one of our founders into key online and print journals. These publications are always looking for ways to satisfy their readers' appetite for thoughtful articles and an offer to write one for free is often quite welcome. The key is to avoid an overt sales pitch. The primary goal is to raise the profile of your company as a thought leader in the industry, not to list the speeds and feeds of your offering. Our PR firm also hit a homerun for us by securing an interview with Linux Magazine that eventually led to RapidMind being the cover story of their monthly print edition. No reader would have guessed that we had a dozen employees and shared a single office phone.

A second approach we used successfully at RapidMind was to out-teach the competition. While bigger competitors were spending money on advertising and trade shows, we were quietly stealing the mindshare of prospects with our information-dense speaking engagements. We were blessed with two founders that were among the most knowledge-able on the topic of parallel programming and were also excellent speakers. We pursued every opportunity we could find to put our founders in front of an audience and impart knowledge. The result was not only thought leadership in the industry but also a stream of leads that we had trouble keeping up with.

A third approach to looking bigger than you are is to partner up. Our early association with IBM and Hewlett-Packard were not only valuable during our fundraising, but dramatically raised our credibility with customers. We were quoted on their press releases; they were quoted on ours; we had free space on their expensive tradeshow booth; we performed joint seminars and webinars. Of course the relationship has to be valuable to both parties, but I couldn't help but feel that we were getting more out of it than they were.

These cost-effective strategies resulted in an industry perception that RapidMind was bigger and far more established than the reality, which helped us with acquiring customers and partners. It's also interesting to note that RIM was also sensitive to the goal of looking bigger than they were. In the early days of BlackBerry, when the adoring press included mentions of Presidential candidate Al Gore and other prominent users, the industry perception of the number of BlackBerry users was far greater than the reality. We kept tight-lipped about our install base until we hit the one million-user mark. And then in a marketing stroke of genius that I can't take credit for, we announced hitting this milestone with the slogan, "2 million thumbs and counting".

Those who like it, like it a lot

As I ponder the Alexander Keith's slogan on the wall of the pub, I finish the impromptu lecture to my hostage by encouraging him to take the leap into entrepreneurship. If you combine your passion for your idea with the collective wisdom of so many in town willing to share… you will indeed like the experience a lot. Proud of my selflessness, I ducked out without paying the bill.

Ray DePaul

Ray has spent his entire 20+ year career in Waterloo successfully bringing high technology products to market. Most recently, Ray was the President & CEO of RapidMind Inc. He joined the University of Waterloo spin-off in 2006 and has steered the company through $11M of venture funding and significant market growth, positioning RapidMind as an industry leader. Ray and his team's efforts culminated in the sale of RapidMind to Intel Corp in August 2009, giving the tech giant its first R&D presence in Ontario.

Prior to RapidMind, Ray spent five years with Research In Motion (RIM) where he was responsible for product management for the iconic BlackBerry product line. Ray helped guide the product through the challenging early adopter stage towards the mainstream market and established the BlackBerry brand as the leader in the wireless data market.

Ray has also played key roles in industries as diverse as consumer electronics, telecommunications, networking, and operating systems. Ray is proud to hold both a Bachelors of Mathematics degree in Computer Science from the University of Waterloo and a Masters of Business Administration from Wilfrid Laurier University, where he is also a frequent guest lecturer on high tech marketing.

Angel Investors:
From Possibility to Probability!

Yvan Couture

One of the most important, yet misunderstood relationships in the tech industry is the one between entrepreneurs and angel investors. When you strip everything away, that relationship can fundamentally be described by the very important transitional objective I like to call going from being a possibility to a probability.

But before we get into what this means, let's get some clarity around the two important players: entrepreneur and angel. It is important to understand that not every person who starts or is involved with a business is an entrepreneur. And not every person who invests in one is an angel investor. Many will have (differing) opinions on how each is defined but for the sake of this piece I'd like to share my thoughts.

The Entrepreneur

Entrepreneur! If there ever was a loaded word with as many definitions as there are people trying to define it, this is it. The Oxford English Dictionary defines it as "a person who sets up a business or businesses". I think the key words here are "who sets up". In fact, the word comes from the French word "entreprendre" which means "to undertake".

I would like to add a bit of colour around that definition in the context of the technology industry.

People will often say that entrepreneurs are people who hear opportunity knocking. Actually, by the time it knocks in tech it is usually too late. Real entrepreneurs are those who hear opportunity whispering; they see things much earlier than everyone else does. It is not that difficult to start a business and build an application or product to fill a hole in an existing, well-defined market. But doing so in uncharted territory (like Mike Lazaridis did with the BlackBerry) is for me the true test. Most tech businesses are started and managed by talented and entrepreneurial people, but only a very few are started by what I would qualify as entrepreneurs.

And please, please stop calling people hired after the business was created entrepreneurs. Case in point! I have been fortunate enough to be associated with three great companies so far; Mitra Imaging (a while back), and today with both Primal and The Official Community

Corporation (OCC). Have I invested in some of these? Yes. Have there been professional and financial risks for me? Yes. Have I taken a "cut in pay" to be involved? Yes. Am I an entrepreneur because of it? A big loud resounding NO!

I certainly have been entrepreneurial, as many others in the tech industry have been, but to call me an entrepreneur because of it takes away from the real ones like Eric Peterson at Mitra, Kevin Leflar at OCC, and my current business partner at Primal, Peter Sweeney.

They heard that whisper; they didn't listen to those who questioned their sanity and continued to persevere; they were the real spark that started these new enterprises. They are the real entrepreneurs. I take nothing away from those who have excelled in helping entrepreneurs build serious, successful businesses. They are important and necessary... but they are not entrepreneurs.

The Angel

Just as not everyone who starts (or is involved with a business) is an entrepreneur, not every investor in an early stage business should be called an angel. Let's not kid ourselves: every dollar raised from any investor is critical to a firm's early success. However, understanding what a "true" angel is helps to put the entrepreneur and angel relationship in perspective.

So what is an angel? Like with "entrepreneurs" there are probably many opinions as to the definition of an "angel". But, again, for the sake of this piece let me outline my thoughts on it.

Angels have significant risk capital available (at least $1 million) to (a) make several investments (or more properly referred to as bets!), and (b) make the inevitable follow-on investments in their portfolio companies. Note that I do not include experience or mentoring capability in this definition as I think both are overrated when assessing the value of an angel. Entrepreneurs need cash. The advice and mentoring, particularly in the Waterloo Region, can be gained from the many sources we have available at the Accelerator Centre, from Communitech, from other entrepreneurs and business people, and from the many great professional services firms. Many angels can provide the advice and mentoring, but it is not necessary when looking for and landing an angel.

Angels, like all other individual or institutional investors everywhere, are not smart enough to pick the winners. And because of that, successful angel investing depends on the ability to make several bets. Success should not be measured by individual investments but rather the overall returns on their portfolio of bets.

Having enough capital to make follow-on investments is critical. As much as the angel and entrepreneur might agree on the project's cash needs it is inevitable that it will take more. You will get the call that payroll won't get covered at month end! And unless you have a reasonable pool of capital to cover it then you may be killing what would otherwise become a successful business. I remember times when I had to write cheques to help cover month ends. In fact, in one case I invested four times more than I had originally intended! And believe me every time you have to make that follow-on decision you realize there is a fine line between looking like an idiot (for throwing good money after bad) or an investing genius (for investing in what could become a success)!

So as you can see, if you are investing the only $25,000 you have available as risk capital it is difficult to call yourself an angel investor. Every dollar raised is critical so let's not discount the value of that hard earned $25,000 investment. But differentiating between being an investor and being an angel investor is important to the discussion of the angel and entrepreneur relationship.

From Possibility to Probability

Now that we have a baseline definition for both the entrepreneur (someone who sets up a business to respond to the whisper they heard) and angel (deep pockets and willingness to make bets) let's discuss this "pact" they make when an investment is made; agreeing to set an objective of going from possibility to probability.

Let's define these two terms first:

Possibility: a future prospect or potential (and for an entrepreneur, the dream)

Probability: a measure of how likely it is that some event (success) will occur

From the initial whisper the entrepreneur outlines the dream about how to answer (and benefit from) that whisper. They then find interested angels (usually one lead angel) and sell them on that dream, that possibility. Angels then decide on making a bet or not on that possibility. By the way, if they ask you for a 3 to 5 year plan... run! Possibilities are just that; something that may be possible based on an opportunity identified. The notion of building a long-term plan at this point is useless, and in fact impossible. Real angels won't ask for this. They will assess the dream, look you in the eyes to see if you have what it takes to go after it, and then make the bet; knowing full well they may lose that money.

The real bet is not made on the possibility *per se*, but rather on the likelihood of the entrepreneur moving it from a possibility to becoming a probability (when you can now put in place execution plans to show

how you will take advantage of the commercial opportunity).

Once a project has moved from just being possible to being probable, it comes down to execution. The entrepreneur's second objective (where the first is moving from possible to probable) is to increase the level of probability of success through execution; building the right team, getting commercial traction, showing growth, etc.

Conclusion

The Region of Waterloo has the makings of a great technology industry entrepreneurial ecosystem. We have a handful of great angels, a growing number of entrepreneurs, outstanding professional services firms (who themselves make bets by providing services at a fraction of their cost to promising new start-ups), and great support provided by Communitech, the Accelerator Centre, our great academic institutions, and much more.

When I say we "have the makings" of a great technology industry entrepreneurial ecosystem I mean that we still have a long way to go to become a global entrepreneurial powerhouse; we need more entrepreneurs, more angels making bets, more Canadian sources of capital to come in after the angels have made their bets, more government support, etc.

A good start! It is now up to us to build on this great foundation.

Yvan Couture

Yvan is an angel investor and is currently CEO, Co-President and Chairman of Primal Fusion Inc. and Chairman of The Official Community Corporation, two companies he has invested in. He is one of the founders of Communitech and has been an active member of the Waterloo tech community since 1991.

How to Tame a Dragon

Andrew Maxwell and Moren Lévesque

Background

Entrepreneurs starting high-potential technology ventures inevitably need to raise equity finance to fund business development in advance of being able to generate revenue. This is because borrowing debt without security is not an option, and the entrepreneur rapidly runs out of his or her own money and that of family and friends. Given the critical nature of raising external funds in the venture creation process, we investigated why most investor-entrepreneur interactions end in failure. One of the intents was to provide practical insights to entrepreneurs for increasing their likelihood of success during such interactions.

Our research started from the perspective that the investment decision is a multi-stage process, with failures at each stage. This allowed us to use a quality improvement approach to identify and then suggest ways to eliminate the causes of failure at each stage. We started by reviewing the literature on new venture investment decision-making and were surprised to find most research only considered venture capitalists – professional fund managers who manage others' investment funds. Given that business angels – individuals who invest their own money - are 30 times more likely to be the source of early stage financing, we decided to focus on their decision-making processes, which have been noted to be quite different from that of venture capitalists.

Others investigating the investment decision-making process had also raised concerns regarding the data collected, particularly because little attention had been paid to the causes of failure. This reduces the chance of identifying prospects for improvement. Also, data on the interaction was often gathered at the end of the decision process, thus limiting our understanding of its stages and relying on foggy investors' recollections that can be subject to hindsight biases. Due to these shortcomings, we decided to develop a research approach that allowed us to directly observe the angel-entrepreneur interactions in real time and focus on why business opportunities were rejected at each process stage. However, interactions between angels and entrepreneurs often take place in private, over a series of confidential meetings, which makes direct observation challenging, especially if concerns are raised that the presence of observers might influence both process and outcome.

Fortuitously, through the Canadian Innovation Centre (in Waterloo) we were asked to help CBC Television develop a new reality-TV show, Dragons' Den. The show's format, which had been developed by the BBC in England, involved hopeful entrepreneurs pitching to a group of five angels – the Dragons – selected based on personality, entrepreneurial experience and willingness to invest. The show's format constrained the interactions in two ways that simplified our research: entrepreneurs either had to be offered all the money originally requested or leave with nothing; and each Dragon had to specify why he or she rejected an opportunity.

Over the first four seasons, the Canadian Innovation Centre worked with the CBC to recruit entrepreneurs, facilitate the audition process, and train selected entrepreneurs how to pitch. About 1500 entrepreneurs auditioned for the show each season, with only 10% invited to the Toronto studio to pitch their business investment opportunities to the Dragons. Involvement in the provision of ongoing assistance to pitching entrepreneurs before and during show taping allowed us to observe at first hand the interactions as they were recorded in real time. We were also able to review the tapes of each interaction, before and after they were edited for TV. Repeated viewing of these tapes to try to explain the reasons for rejection enabled us to recognize certain patterns in the interactions. It also encouraged us to consider using these interactions for our research, because they overcame some of the data-collection limitations previously identified.

Our involvement in this reality-TV show (to confirm the genuineness of the interactions and enable access to the unedited tapes) convinced key members of the research community that, despite some concerns, valuable insights on the real-time investment decisions of angels could be gathered. An initial analysis of the investment decision-making process showed the multi-stage nature of the investment decision process and that criteria considered when rejecting an opportunity differed from one stage to the next. Repeated views of interactions enabled us to develop behavioural coding schema for each stage of the process to seek evidence to support hypotheses developed based on our understanding of decision-making under risk. Our hypotheses suggest the investment decision is a multistage process with different criteria considered at each stage.

In this chapter, we highlight some of our key findings and their practical implications for investors, entrepreneurs and stakeholders interested in increasing the success rates of investor-entrepreneur interactions. Those involved in the investment process will not be surprised to find out that, in addition to the extant research in entrepreneurship and financing, we drew on research from behavioral economics and social psychology to hypothesize about the decision-making process and the relative importance of certain criteria in the rejection decisions at each stage. We now share some of our findings.

Business Angel Decision Making

Figure 7 identifies four distinct stages of the investment decision process, with the angel using different cognitive processes at each to either reject the business opportunity or allow it to proceed to the subsequent stage. Rejection rates are high early in the process to minimize the amount of time spent looking at opportunities of limited interest (leaving more time to investigate the remaining opportunities at later stages in the process). Experienced investors develop heuristics to minimize the cognitive effort required in complex decision-making. In a multi-stage process, the amount of effort the angel is willing to spend and the number of criteria considered increases as the interaction progresses. While the consideration of only a limited number of criteria as reason for early rejection reduces decision accuracy, it seems the angel is willing to compromise accuracy for expediency.

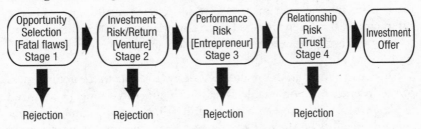

Figure 7: Staged investment decision-making process

During the *first stage* (Stage 1), we observed that *the presence of a single fatal flaw* provided a sufficient reason for rejection. This decision-making technique, known as "Elimination-By-Aspects," is an efficient filtering approach when the decision-maker has to select a few out of a large pool of opportunities. The decision-maker's cognitive effort was minimized, since he or she simply had to identify a fatal flaw in any one of the eight critical factors listed in Table 1 as sufficient reason for rejection. Each of these factors was found to be non-compensatory; a high rating in one could not compensate for a low rating in another. A non-compensatory technique minimizes cognitive effort as no effort is wasted analyzing interactions between factors.

Table 1: Critical Factors and Potential Fatal Flaws

Critical Factor	Fatal flaw
Product adoption	No evidence potential customers likely to adopt
Route to market	No clear channel to market
Product development status	Much more research and development required
Market potential	Market size too small
Protectability	No barrier to entry for competitors
Customer engagement	Features do not match market need
Relevant experience	No relevant entrepreneurial / business experience
Financial model	No clear path to profitability

Once the investor had confirmed both the absence of a fatal flaw and no conflict with his or her personal investment objectives,[16] the opportunity moved to the *second stage* (Stage 2), where the angels undertook a *venture assessment* to determine if the investment return and risk exceeded his or her personal investment thresholds. The investment return is the angel's anticipated return based on an estimation of the venture value at exit. The investment risk is the angel's assessment of the likelihood that the business will fail before this exit point is reached (typically 5-8 years). Should the angel's threshold level for investment return not be achieved, or the threshold level for acceptable risk exceeded, the angel will reject the opportunity without further consideration.

To reject an opportunity at this stage due to insufficient investment return, the angel analyzed disclosed information and forecasts about revenues (based on customer adoption and market growth) and profitability (based on route to market and protectability) to predict future venture value. This estimate of the future venture value was influenced by the angel's knowledge of the market as well as the identification of potential acquirers. Although the criteria considered at that stage were similar to those considered at the previous stage, the critical factors in Table 1 were now used in a compensatory manner when determining future venture value and investment return. This compensatory technique required more cognitive effort than at the previous stage in order to determine if the threshold level of expected return would be achieved.

---

[16] The presence of five investors removed personal objectives from our research, as they were rarely consistent among investors, and we coded based on the last Angel to reject the opportunity.

For an assessment of the investment risk, the angel considered the *performance risk* and the *relationship risk*. The performance risk is the risk that the company will not achieve its objectives, while the relationship risk is the risk that the entrepreneur will not act in the best long-term interests of the angel. Given the assessment of performance risk takes less effort than the assessment of the relationship risk, it was assessed earlier in the process. The inherent performance risk[17] includes both internal and external risk, as exemplified in Table 2, where increases in risk increase the likelihood the venture will fail. These risks can be: financial (adoption rates/market size), technology (product development), physical (supply chain) and managerial (strategic partners).

Table 2: Performance Risk

Risk Dimension	Internal Aspects	External Aspects
Financial	High development costs, low gross margins, negative cash flow	Customer insolvency, economic stability, venture funds
Technical	Technology failure, production challenges, development delays	Competitor actions, supplier challenges, external innovation
Physical	Plant infrastructure, operational challenges, infrastructure	Material sourcing, supply chain challenges, logistics issues
Managerial	Dysfunctional or unbalanced team, experience issues	Market changes, recruitment challenges, partner problems

We observed that the rejection decision, based on the opportunity not reaching investment risk and return thresholds, was non-compensatory. In other words, shortfalls in investment return could not compensate for lower levels of risk, and vice versa. An explanation of the non-compensatory nature of these factors can be found in neuro economics, where MRI brain scans show investment return and risk to be analyzed in different areas of the brain. As the brain struggles to reconcile conflicts between these two areas, heuristics encourage individuals to consider each separately.

During the *third stage* (Stage 3), the investor considered the effect of the entrepreneur's *anticipated behaviour* on the *performance risk*: specifically, whether or not behaviours seen as manifestations of certain types of characteristics could decrease the likelihood of receiving an investment offer. The effect of these entrepreneurial behaviours on performance risk

---

17 Inherent performance risk is the venture's performance risk before the impact of the entrepreneur is considered.

could only be seen once the inherent performance risk (i.e., from the venture) was understood. As shown in Table 3, we identified three types of entrepreneurial *characteristics*– capabilities, experiences and traits– manifested as behaviors that affected the performance risk, noting that the angel's assessment of each type could increase the performance risk above that angel's risk threshold and cause the opportunity to be rejected.

Table 3: Entrepreneur Characteristics

Characteristic Type	Facets
Capabilities	Competence, Critical Thinking, New Venture Skill
Experience	Prior Activities, Relevant Knowledge, Education
Traits	Emotional Stability, Extraversion, Openness (to experience), Agreeableness, Conscientiousness

We found that behaviours that indicated higher levels of capabilities and experiences increased the likelihood of receiving an offer, although above a certain level, higher levels of experience[18] had limited impact on this likelihood. We also observed that manifestations of behaviors linked to individual traits had an inverted-U shaped relationship with the likelihood of receiving an offer. For each of the five traits in Table 3, the entrepreneur had to display sufficient, but not excess manifestations of each trait (e.g., too little extraversion would reduce confidence in the entrepreneur's ability, while too much extraversion could reduce decision-making quality). Behaviors that were manifestations of the three types of characteristics were independent of the angels and thus easier for them to assess. Since they required less cognitive effort, they were examined before any entrepreneurial behaviors specific to the angel-entrepreneur relationships.

During the *final stage* (Stage 4), the angel had to have confidence that the entrepreneur would make decisions in that angel's best interests (e.g., not spend development money on a "pet project"). The assessment of this *relationship risk* required greater cognitive effort, as the angel had to use his or her own experience and evidence from behaviours manifested during the interaction to anticipate how the long-term relationship might develop. Angels aware that such relationships often exceeded five years viewed the investment decision not only from a financial perspective, but also from an emotional one.

We observed that the relationship risk was assessed based on the development of a trust-based relationship with the entrepreneur. We

---

[18]   Limited positive effect of higher experience levels on investment decision could be due to entrenchment effects that can limit adaptability and thought processes and limit the quality of decision-making.

found that trust development was linked to the manifestations of four types of trust-based behaviors, as identified in Table 4, that could each build, damage or violate trust.[19] These trust-based behaviors include trusting (showing vulnerability), trustworthy (confirming the decision to trust), being capable (confirming claimed ability) and communicative (free flow of information). Manifestations of each behavior increased the likelihood that the entrepreneur would receive an investment offer, while behaviors that damaged or violated trust reduced that likelihood. We also found that, while damaged trust could be repairable through the introduction of control mechanisms (e.g., Angel's direct participation in venture), violated trust destroyed further relationship development.

Table 4: Entrepreneur's Trust-Based Behaviors

Behavior	Facets
Trusting	Disclosure, Reliance, Receptiveness
Trustworthy	Consistent, Benevolent, Alignment
Capable	Competence, Experience, Judgment
Communicative	Accuracy, Explanation, Openness (timely disclosure)

Practical Insight for Fund-Seeking Entrepreneurs

Our findings provide some guidance to entrepreneurs who wish to increase their chance of receiving an investment offer. Entrepreneurs can try to eliminate fatal flaws prior to meeting with an angel, or communicate how potential concerns can be addressed. Should this not be possible, a better understanding of why the eight critical factors offered in Table 1 are important might stimulate an entrepreneur to redirect his or her energy to a different opportunity or career path.

Understanding how angels use investment return and risk thresholds when making investment decisions can help entrepreneurs provide information to reassure the investor that risk can be reduced or external resources accessed. Conscious that specific behaviours may increase performance risk, the entrepreneur can recruit team members with complementary characteristics that make up for shortcomings, or partner with individuals who can mitigate the entrepreneur's trait excesses and reduce risk. For example, to attract investors, entrepreneurs need to be passionate about their business, however excessive displays of passion, such as refusing to relinquish some control of the venture, can have a negative effect on potential relationships. Finally, trust is crucial to

---

[19]   The difference between behaviors that damage or violate trust is based on behavioral intent: trust can be damaged by ignorance but violated through deception.

attract investment and develop long-term relationships. Awareness of how certain trust-based behaviours influence relationships can increase the likelihood of successful outcomes and focus attention on meeting the financial and emotional needs of partners.

Andrew Maxwell

Andrew Maxwell has an engineering degree (Imperial College) and an MBA (London Business School) and started his career working for technology multinationals, in Europe and North America. Attracted by the lure of an entrepreneurial activity he joined an environmental service company where he cofounded an environmental technology business. His entrepreneurial experience proved invaluable in helping develop several start-ups including: wireless, medical device and web companies. This experience led him to join the University of Toronto's Technology Transfer Office where he founded its technology incubator – the Exceler@tor, home to 30 technology businesses. In addition to teaching Technology Entrepreneurship at the University of Waterloo, Andrew is completing a Ph.D. there in venture creation. His specific interest is in the identification of diagnostic factors that can separate ventures that succeed from those that fail. He has presented his research globally and has a number of academic and business publications in leading academic journals. In his spare time, Andrew works at the Canadian Innovation Centre where, among other activities, he presents a monthly webinar for technology entrepreneurs and has been an industry advisor to CBC Dragons' Den.

Moren Lévesque

Moren Lévesque is an Associate Professor at the Schulich School of Business, York University. She holds a Ph.D. in Management Science from the University of British Columbia and M.Sc., B.Sc. in Mathematics from Université Laval. Moren's faculty positions include: Carnegie Mellon University, Rensselaer Polytechnic Institute, Case Western Reserve University, and most recently at the University of Waterloo as a Canada Research Chair in Innovation & Technical

Entrepreneurship. Her teaching areas have included operations research, and entrepreneurship at the undergraduate and graduate levels. Her research applies the methodologies of analytical and quantitative disciplines to the study of decision making in new business formation. Her work appears in *Entrepreneurship Theory and Practice, IEEE Transactions on Engineering Management Journal of Business Venturing* and *Organization Science*, among other research outlets. She is a senior editor at *Production and Operations Management*, and as a member of the Research Committee at the Academy of Management's Entrepreneurship Division. Her research has been featured in popular press, including: Business Times, The Record, The Globe and Mail, National Post, and PROFIT Magazine.

A working couple's guide to reducing stress

Ann Zimmer

Many couples, where both partners work, face added challenges when organizing daily life, trying to spend time together and manage stress. When one of the partners is a CEO and faces the added stress and responsibility this job entails, it adds further complications. In our family, we have discovered, through trial and error, that many small actions can make life much easier, allowing us to support one another and reduce stress, both at home and at the office.

Timing is Everything: Scheduling

It would be nice if we could plan our lives and have everything work out as planned, however this is hardly ever the case. CEOs have many demands on their time and cannot work the often desired 9 to 5. Their schedule is likely to change over the course of the day and last minute delays are inevitable, causing not only work but also home stress. Last minute changes can be as simple as a meeting running late, or waiting for an important fax, to complications such as employee questions, client demands and problems or a human resources crisis. Having a plan to limit the effect on those at home can help reduce stress for both parties.

This unpredictable schedule often leads to burnt suppers and frustrated partners. Some strategies we employ to handle this issue: use respect, communication and advance planning. One of the first things we did was to develop the 15 minute rule. If either of us was running more than 15 minutes late, we were to call or email the other as soon as possible and let them know. This meant fewer burnt suppers and a better ability for the other partner to adjust his or her plans. Another strategy we developed for days when it is important to be home on time is to have no meeting planned during the last half hour of work and to let key employees know in advance that you will be unavailable after a certain time. Another idea is to let your partner know when you have meetings at the end of the day- sort of advance warning that you maybe late.

We also found that scheduling out-of-office appointments (i.e., doctor) work best first thing in the morning, when they are still on schedule, or last thing in the evening, it's always a good idea to call and check if they're running late - better to spend an extra few minutes at work instead of in the waiting room. If I set up an appointment of this type, I make sure it gets entered into the schedule, especially for daytime appointments. I also try to send reminder emails during the day if there is an unusual activity planned for the evening.

To help out, on days when meetings are likely to run late, plan a more flexible meal – one that won't burn or dry out if your partner runs late. I have also found that when coordinating events, I try to make reasonable requests and determine which events are must-attend versus optional. I often check to see how busy the schedule already is that day or week (i.e., if travelling on the schedule) and then decide if it's worth mentioning. If work permits, it can be easier to get remote access to an electronic schedule – it can be set up with viewing and/or writing privileges. For must-attend events, I am usually prepared to attend alone, if that's how things work out. I also try to have back-ups available, whom I can call on in an emergency for things like child care, in case one of us is running late. I am fortunate enough to have my in-laws near enough that my mother-in-law can step in with two hours notice.

Can I just... Interruptions and Distractions

I remember once hearing somewhere that every interruption results in an hour and a half of diminished efficiency. A CEO's day is constantly filled with interruptions from employees looking for advice, to unexpected client phone calls and handling crises – in many cases these interruptions cannot be avoided. However, there are ways to limit some interruptions.

There are often times throughout the week when I need to call my partner for various reasons, and after interrupting a few employee/client meetings, we developed a system that reduces undesirable distractions. In an emergency, we can call anytime, but for random everyday calls I send an email – stating "call when free". I include times I will be unavailable if I have any upcoming meetings in the next two hours. This works really well, not only do I not interrupt him, I get more of his attention when he does call, usually within half an hour.

Other distractions involve the undesirable effects of having to run odd chores just before or after work, something as simple as getting your car serviced can be extremely frustrating when the service centre calls to confirm a quote or get approval for extra work. Getting back to pick up the car can cause serious problems, clients don't react well to being rushed off the phone when it's time for your pick up.

I am fortunate in that my work place is fairly flexible, I can arrive a little late or leave a little early, and even work from home on occasion - as long as I make up the time later in the week. This flexibility in my schedule means I am able to take a lot of odd chores on my plate. I am the one responsible for getting the cars to and from the garage for servicing and for dealing with service personnel (i.e., furnace or a/c service) at home. The trade-off is that my husband does the research for major purchases (i.e., which new furnace to buy) and handles most of the complaint calls. He also does a little extra around the house on the weekend on those occasions where handling these chores results in my having to work a few hours on the weekend to make up for lost time at work. This strategy works well, since as CEO he can't be late for client meetings and often can't control when they are scheduled. A few minutes of extra work on my part handling these situations takes a great deal of potential stress out of the CEO's day.

One other thing – a good night's sleep is very important. If you can do it, turn off your phone or at least the e-mail notifications from 11 pm to 7 am. Most things can wait until morning, the extra rest will allow you to make better decisions.

It's not just for work anymore: Delegation

One of the first things a CEO learns is that they cannot do everything themselves and that they need to delegate. A CEO does not work the normal 9 to 5, in fact they work pretty much all the time, including from home, in the car, on vacation... To actually get some free time it is important to delegate while at home too. When both partners work, this means outside help may be required.

When we moved from our apartment to a house, we discovered there was a drastic increase in the number of things that needed to get done every week. We felt it was important to spend quality time together and decided that we didn't want that time eaten up doing chores. It was time to delegate. We hired a housekeeper to come in every other week and hired a lawn care company during the summer. We use the time we save to do some of our favourite things, such as going to movies, hiking, and just hanging out together. This leaves us both more relaxed and in better moods to handle the stresses of our jobs.

A family that plays together: Planning

CEOs tend to do a lot of travelling in their jobs, visiting clients, going on sales calls, and attending conferences. All this travelling takes a toll on the family, the CEO is tired from coming and going and the family missing out on spending time together. When possible, it is a good idea to delegate some of the travel, but this is not always possible, so you should try to make the best of it. The first thing I did was write a travel check list and post it on our notice board. This was the result of my husband reaching the airport once without a passport, and another time without the booth for a trade show. Whenever preparing for a business trip, this list is consulted and double-checked before heading out the door. The original list has been added to and modified over time and now things are rarely forgotten. We have become very efficient travellers.

As my husband's role has changed over the years, he has to do a lot more business trips. This makes planning activities, spending time together and scheduling vacations even harder. In our case, once every few months I try to join him on one of his trips and we extend it out a few days and over the weekend. We explore the area and do all the normal touristy things. We even took our 6 week old to California, where my husband was attending a conference. We spent the weekend exploring the nearby parks. We do the same on some of my work trips, where we spent a few days exploring Switzerland. The important thing to remember is that during the working segment, work comes first: the visiting partner must be respectful of this – most evenings during this segment of the trip will require some work as well – a good book is always an ideal solution for these evenings.

Staying Sane: Respect

There are many challenges faced by the daily lives of a working couple, the most important aspect of getting through those days together and happy is respect. All of the above challenges and solutions work well in our family, we have learned to balance needs against desires and found ways to spend more time together. We respect each other and the time it takes to do our jobs well, when we spot an opening for improvement or ways to help, we do that.

These actions can be as small as sleeping in the guest room when you're sick to keep the other person healthy, emptying the dishwasher, or offering to watch the children to give your spouse an unexpected hour of quiet time after a stressful day. Each little thing we do for one another helps to reduce our stress, make us feel loved and gives us the motivation we need to be successful every day.

Be respectful of one another, be supportive of each other and look for ways to make your lives easier so that you can spend your time wisely.

Ann Zimmer

Ann Zimmer has a Ph.D. in Computer Science and a M. Math in Pure Math from the University of Waterloo. She received her B.Sc. from Bishop's University with an Honours in Mathematics and a Major in Computer Science. She is currently working as a software developer designing industrial automation solutions.

Corporate Culture: Finding Your Epic

Brydon Gilliss

When BandOfCoders began, it wasn't a band of anything, in fact it was a small consulting shop named MDC Consulting. Besides the founding partners, it was made up primarily of myself and a polite Christian named Drew who had nine kids and lived on a farm in Texas.

My partners and I had plans. This was a company, a unique company unlike all those other crappy companies. No gray cubicles, no managers, no offices, dogs everywhere, free pop, pints, candy, video games. We were the epitome of 2.0 before the world knew about 2.0. We were a different company, or at least we planned on it.

Knowing I wanted to help create a unique company is, well, not all that unique. I had no idea how to create and maintain this so-called different company. It struck me earlier this year while attending a software conference just how boring and common this mission is. While I sat and listened to a day full of talks, the consistent refrain was the call to be different. Do something different, create a different company. In the social events that evening I didn't bump into any founders building a common, boring software company. We would all be different. The problem was: we were all the same.

In 2008 I stepped away from the daily project work with BandOfCoders in order to help a new start-up named Brainpark. Once again we had no intention of being boring or the same. From our products to our marketing to our daily office happenings, we had every intent of building yet another *different* company. Once again we had no idea what we were doing but we knew what we disliked about these companies that weren't different.

Brainpark and BandOfCoders are two of a gaggle of companies I've been lucky enough to work directly with over the last decade plus. Not only were each of those businesses unique, they were all moving targets, shifting daily under the stresses placed upon them by technology, economy, customers, markets, family etc. There are surprisingly few concrete lessons to be learned that are directly transferable through the life of a company. There's some irony in writing this in a book titled *The Entrepreneurial Effect: Waterloo* but reading books on the subject does little to prepare you. What will prepare you is realizing that experience counts. By experience, I don't mean listing previous jobs on your resume,

I'm talking what I've come to refer to as *epics*.

In rock climbing, it's recognized that to grow as a climber you need to accumulate *epics*. So much so that it's part of the language. You'll speak with someone and hear them explicitly say, "did I tell you about the epic we experienced last weekend at Joshua Tree?" Epics are notches on your belt you have to seek out and acquire.

In 2005, Lynn Hill and a much younger Katie Brown made the first female free-ascent of the West Face, Leaning Tower, Yosemite. When Lynn spoke about taking this challenge on with Katie, she said that "Yosemite is a place where you have to have had a certain number of experiences and epics before you really understand what you're getting into."

While reading, schooling, studying to gain skills is still a large part of climbing, no one's naive enough to think they can become a great, or even a good, climber through books, mentors, and classrooms alone. It's a given that climbers who fear and avoid getting themselves into epics will never gain the experience needed to be great. Chess is the same in that, to become great, you need a balance of experiences gained through playing real games and studying.

In rock climbing, choosing your climbing partners can be a life and death decision. You have to climb with people you feel you can survive epics with. People not only skilled but able to communicate effectively with you. People willing to have the tough conversations required after epics that allow you all to learn and move on to the next.

Experiencing an epic is only the beginning. The tough part follows, which is where the growth occurs. Back at the camp site, reflecting on what happened on the cliff that day. "Next time we should try this, that worked when you called out that to me but next time let's try this." In climbing, it's understood that you must be light, fast, with minimal protection. You excel based on "your wits, your experience and the strength of your companions."[20]

In a lot of ways, our instinct in business can be the opposite. We strive to avoid epics and we over-protect each other from them. When you hear people speak of failing fast and failing early and often, clearly they aren't suggesting you fail on purpose. They want you get out there and earn your epics, most of which will be indistinguishable from failure in the early days. That's the key point. Epics and failures look almost identical in the early days. What is counter-intuitive is that individuals and businesses alike need to seek out their own epics.

So what am I rambling about and how does it relate to entrepreneur-

---

[20]   Adam J. Wolf, retrieved 2011/06/01 from www.ydnar.com/

ship? To me, what sets entrepreneurs apart from all others is loneliness. You've left the tribe and headed down your own path and there are no manuals or guidebooks. In most cases no one's experienced what you're tackling today.

Of course you need valued mentors but they aren't enough. Mentors "provide expertise to less experienced individuals to help them advance their careers"[21]. When you're blazing trails and creating something from nothing, there is no one more experienced than you. What Lynn and Katie did in Yosemite that day had never been done before. Recognizing that you need to seek out your epics requires that you surround yourself with the right tribe. You need a support structure to help you live through your epics, learn all you can from them, prepare for your next epic and go find it.

If you're going after epics then I'd challenge you to build real diversity into your tribe. You need people who ground you personally and are willing to call you task and have the ugly conversations. It's all too easy for us to distance ourselves from people who challenge our ideas. Find people who are able to separate the business from personal. Someone who can tear your idea to shreds, leave you curled up in the corner and then pick you up and take you for a pint to plan out your next epic. Too often we surround ourselves with those like-minded folks who agree with and offer only approval and validation. Recognize that surrounding yourself with people who validate everything you do offers you nothing.

We have a natural inclination to drift towards sameness in who we surround ourselves with. Clearly we connect with people more like us and this flocking nature can leave us surrounded by like-minded people, and not necessarily in a good way. I'm not sure who said it but I quote it often: "if two people always agree then one person is redundant."

In Youngme Moon's recent book *Different*, she explains this phenomenon in relation to companies and brands but it strikes me that advisors are no different. In seeking valued advice from experienced mentors, we often find ourselves lacking real diversity. She describes how brands tend to focus on improving their weaknesses in relation to their direct competitors. She introduces the notion of doubling down on your brand's strengths, and accepting your weaknesses as a way to truly differentiate your brand.

I find we take a similar approach with our mentors and advisors. You're strong at front end technology and building a community around you. You're weak at sales, marketing and database layer. The obvious approach is to find mentors strong at sales, marketing and backend development.

My experience is this. When given the choice of who you work with or who your advisors and tribe are, I use this little test. If shit literally hits

---

[21] www.wikipedia defintion of mentor, accessed 2011/06/01

the fan tomorrow, who do I want to be in the room with? That's what an epic is; it's the roof caving in. Think of those epics: your only client leaves, half your team quits, think of the equivalent of an earthquake in your business, now who do you want in the room to help you survive? When epics engulf you, there are no simple answers, there are only difficult questions and problems. Surviving them isn't about what books you've read and how you've prepared, it's about immediate action today.

So I encourage you to get out there and find your own epics. Grow your tribe and surround yourself with people willing to challenge you, your ideas and your actions. Being an entrepreneur isn't all that different from climbing, you need to survive and learn from tomorrow's epic and repeat.

Brydon Gilliss

If career success in software were simply defined as the design and development of innovative and intuitive software, then Brydon Gilliss would be very successful. Since the late 90s, after earning an Honours B.Sc. in Engineering Systems and Computing from the University of Guelph, he's been the lead developer of new technologies and software for companies like Cognicase (formerly Personus), MKS Inc, and his current assignment as Product Manager of Brainpark, where his thoughtful design and expert development of product customizations earned him Communitech's Annual Tech Impact Award in the fall of 2009.

But to Brydon, an equally important component to success is supporting and contributing to a strong and viable tech community on a local level. It's this commitment to his industry that prompted Brydon to launch DemoCampGuelph, an informal and collaborative meeting of 100+ minds for those in and around the Guelph area involved in any and all aspects of the web, software, start-ups, and tech. Additionally, Brydon has been recognized within the industry for helping local entrepreneurs develop and advance innovative ideas.

To add to his list of accomplishments, Brydon has been asked to share his knowledge and enthusiasm for the tech industry with a number of speaking engagements that have included meshU, DemoCampToronto, Guelph Technology Organization, Guelph Technology Economy, and more.

When the workday is over, Brydon enjoys spending time with his wife and two children, passing the puck, and wielding any number of power tools renovating his downtown Guelph home.

The importance of workplace culture

Dave Caputo

I have the privilege to work with my friends every single day. I am not sure that many people in today's workforce can say those words and truly mean it. But I can. And I can because Sandvine has a truly distinct culture, one that resonates with every team member and is reinforced with every team meeting, group project and management technique. I believe a healthy and happy work environment is a gift we give ourselves and that no matter how good a product or service is or how competitive your pricing is, a winning organization is only as strong as its winning team – and success will come to those who have created a culture that everyone can get behind.

Sandvine didn't grow into its culture. Sandvine's culture was engineered.

I was inspired early on in my career after attending a lecture by Wharton Professor Peter Capelli that made me really think about the net affects of culture in the workforce. At that point in my career, it was a real surprise learning that the primary key to holding talent was built on friendship and trusted relationships. Peter's lecture highlighted two truths about retaining top talent in organizations. He reinforced that the number one reason that motivates people to leave an organization: "I hate my boss" and the number one reason that engenders people to stay: "I work with my friends". It was then that I learned the secret sauce to creating a winning team.

Sandvine's culture was deliberately engineered on day one of business. In developing what we call "The Sandvine Way", we pooled together all of the positive and negative experiences we had had in previous jobs and created a wish list of how we'd like to work together. It is important to note, that we didn't reinvent the wheel for everything, we kept in place policies or practices that worked well in other organizations, namely HP and Cisco. It wasn't about creating the new math, but doing what was fundamentally right and holding ourselves to the highest standards.

We started the process with the founder's recurrent theme of committing to make Sandvine "a fun place to work". Building on past job experience's, we all agreed this commitment would be the foundation of Sandvine. From there, we built out our mission and goals (we can't just be a fun place, everyone has to be on the same page for what we are trying to achieve), management fundamentals (no reinventing the wheel on best practices… "what was Cisco's expense report policy?") and a specific section dedicated to people managers called "Leaders' Ten Commandments" (managers have to be held to a higher standard as they might be the number one reason top talent have left organizations.)

We fleshed out the entire Sandvine Way culture and haven't changed it since inception. We still use the same Sandvine Way slide as we did on day one.

Sandvine's secret sauce–The Sandvine Way

The Sandvine Way has eight tenets that represent our values and beliefs and dictate how we interact with each other. Team members are introduced to The Sandvine Way as a part of their initial new hire training and are reintroduced to it each year on their birthday month.

Table 5 The Sandvine Way

➤ **Customer First** • Make them Successful	➤ **Teamwork** • Work Hard/Play Hard
➤ **Showcase Flexibility** • Make them Successful	➤ **Knowledge Sharing** • Over Communicate/Learning Environment, Design Reviews
➤ **Under Promise/Over Deliver** • Aggressively Promise but make Commitment	➤ **Zero Politics** • Do the Right Thing. Everything else will take care of itself
➤ **Amazing Tool Utilization** • Issue tracking, revision control, intranet…	➤ **Risk Taking** • 3 out of 4 is better than 2 out of 2

Each tenet holds much meaning to our organization and I could give numerous examples for each.

I will highlight three of our tenets here.

Customer First: This is an extremely important tenet and was critical early-on in our success. As a small start-up firm selling to multi-million dollar service providers, there was a real risk associated with customers investing in us. I used to joke with our sales team that "No one ever got fired buying IBM or Cisco". IBM is an industry giant, the safe bet. Buying from a start-up company that is new to the market and offering leading-edge technology can be seen as quite the risk. So building trust early on and ensuring customer success was the foundation of our initial sales strategy. We had to give these initial customers a reason to go out on a limb and try something new, try the new start-up Sandvine technology. We rewarded those customers (and ourselves) by ensuring each customer looked like a star to his/her internal team. Our job was/ is to make sure they are successful which directly affects our successes.

Knowledge sharing: At Sandvine, we hold bi-weekly *Breakfast Peer Topics* that anyone across the organization can attend and any team member can present at. Providing an environment where people share information helps build relationships and efficiencies and reduces mistakes. It is human nature to want to learn from each other so we foster that natural ability. It is also a great way to cross-functionally introduce team members and provide tools for people to better do their jobs. I attended a lunch and learn the other week on "Developing Expertise", where one of our top engineers used the analogy of his quest to become a world-ranked scrabble player and wow, if I had had some of that knowledge earlier in my career, it would have really helped me out.

Another great example is **Risk Taking**: This tenet was generated from situations in previous organizations where team members weren't empowered to make decisions, ultimately because they weren't empowered to make mistakes. Similar to learning and growing in everyday life, you have to allow yourself to fall down once in a while! No one ever sets out to make a bad decision; in fact the only way you ever realize that you make a bad decision is when new information presents itself showing you a better approach. At Sandvine we recognize the importance of developing decision makers; people who aren't afraid to make good decisions in the face of making a bad one once in a while. So long as you don't get involved in hiding a mistake and always learn from it, why block that process and punish people for growing? We are here to promote decision-making and taking risks.

Engineered to last

Most marketing strategists will tell you that it is important to reinforce and repeat messages often to really make them stick. We employ the same tactic with our Sandvine Way principles. The Sandvine Way tenets are found throughout our organization—they are printed in everyone's lab book, displayed in the lunchroom, on the back of ID cards and presented at each company meeting.

We kick-off company meetings by recognizing employees who embody The Sandvine Way. Customer success stories and entertaining and inspirational workplace stories that embody The Sandvine Way tenets and reinforce behaviors that help us stay accountable to our culture. These stories are often told by one team member about another and become the legends that reinforce the reality.

The success of engineering our culture? The proof is in the pudding.

We are measured on an annual basis through Great Places to Work Institute Canada, an organization that works with The Globe and Mail to publish the Best Workplaces in Canada List. Throughout all of Sandvine's successes, my favorite award is continuing to win, year after year, a spot on Canada's best places to work survey.

Sandvine: 350 team members strong

When we first started Sandvine and The Sandvine Way we were comprised of only 20 team members. It was really easy to keep the culture real and alive. The entire organization could fit into a boardroom for monthly meetings; we all knew each other and recognized new hires in the hallways; and we were all located in one building.

Now Sandvine is 350 team members strong, doing business in over 80 countries and we are keeping our culture as consistent as possible. Every team member, from Waterloo to United Kingdom to Hong Kong will start their employment at Sandvine's head office learning about our products, solutions and corporate culture. After nine years of Sandvine Way presentations, I still personally give the monthly three-hour presentation to each group of new hires that joins our team. And, having the birthday month "re-indoctrinations", really allows the new folks to see it isn't something we just talk about, but actually live. The Sandvine Way is a mirror we get to reflect upon ourselves and ask "Am I making the company better because I am a part of it?"

I regularly invite people to quit if they don't believe in trying to achieve The Sandvine Way and no one has ever taken me up on it; on the contrary it is consistently, the number one thing that folks tell me that inspires them most about being on Team Sandvine.

Making the Internet better

Sandvine is in the business of making the Internet better–and that starts within the borderless Sandvine walls. You can't build a great product if you don't have a great team and you can't have a great team if you don't share a common vision and values. At Sandvine we are all proud to say we work with our friends and I feel lucky to be a part of that each and every day.

If I can give one piece of advice to future entrepreneurs, it would be to pay close attention to creating and sustaining your corporate culture. It is by far the most important piece of business a future leader can influence.

You know, when you work with your friends, it hardly feels like work at all.

Dave Caputo

Dave is co-founder, president and CEO at Sandvine.

Dave is responsible for leading an enthusiastic team of professionals who are committed to protecting and improving the quality of experience on the Internet.

Prior to co-founding Sandvine, Dave was the vice president of marketing for PixStream—which was later sold to Cisco Systems for more than $500 million. At Cisco, Dave was the managing director for the video networking business unit and was formerly the product marketing manager at Hewlett Packard.

In 2007, Dave and his fellow co-founders were honoured with the Ernst and Young Entrepreneur of the Year award in the technology category for their success and dedication to their work at Sandvine.

As a leader in the technology community, Dave is a dedicated supporter of local entrepreneurs and speaks regularly at universities. Dave is also on the Board of Communitech, a regional organization that supports the growth of the technology sector.

Dave holds an MBA from the University of Toronto, a computer science degree from York University and is a graduate of Wharton executive education.

The Future of Digital Content

Tom Jenkins—author, entrepreneur and business leader in the technology sector for over 20 years—writes about how to securely manage the explosion of digital content in the enterprise. *Managing Content in the Cloud* describes the evolution of Internet technologies, from early search engines and team collaboration tools to text mining, immersive environments, social media and mobile access to content. Over 50 organizations are profiled to demonstrate solutions in action.

Get your copy today! www.opentext.com/ecmbook

Tom Jenkins is Executive Chairman and Chief Strategy Officer for OpenText. Under his leadership, the Company has grown into a global leader in Enterprise Content Management and Canada's largest software company. OpenText brings two decades of expertise supporting 100 million users in 114 countries.

OPENTEXT
THE CONTENT EXPERTS

TEST YOUR ENTREPRENEURIAL CAPABILITY

After reading the book of articles filled with lessons learned, the final section provides a case study of an entrepreneurial company.

This case was developed to be used in the entrepreneurship stream of a university case competition. Students are given three hours to read, analyze and prepare a presentation on their recommendations.

In the following section we have provided both the case and judge's notes. I suggest you read the case, think how you would deal with the situation and then review the judge's notes. Did you come up with the same solution? Are the judge's notes correct?

Good luck

The Shopify Case

James Bowen, Aurélien Leftick and Harley Finkelstein

"Sellers will be able to create a very professional multi-page website with little or no programming skills in just a few minutes."
– Mike Arrington, Editor in Chief, Techcrunch

Tobias Lütke is the CEO of recent start-up called Shopify (the "company"). He, Harley Finkelstein, Chief Platform Officer, and, Aurélien Leftick in charge of sales strategies, were deep in conversation concerning several strategic possibilities.

Tobias was a co-founder of Shopify. He started his career as a programmer and is now concerned with technical and strategic issues facing the company. Harley Finkelstein is an entrepreneur and lawyer, who has a background in start-ups and eCommerce. Aurélien had graduated with a business degree within the last decade and focused on sales-related issues.

Shopify is a web application that provides the functionality for businesses to create an online store. Shopify was built using *Ruby on Rails*, an open source web application framework. Shopify was launched in May 2006.

The platform is designed to provide the functionality needed for individuals and organizations to sell online, including a product inventory management and order management system, as well as content management, and payment system connections. The Shopify application store offers additional features and applications from third party developers.

Users of the platform have full access to the CSS and HTML capabilities, and can use the templating engine to customize their storefronts. Shopify is proprietary software and currently only available in English.

In December 2009, Shopify launched the $100,000 "Build a Business" contest. Contestants used the Shopify platform to create an online store and the winners were selected based on their two best selling months. This contest generated a great deal of publicity and many new customers, potential customers and those just curious about online stores. The Shopify revenue numbers showed a clear and sustaining jump correlated to the contest.

In addition to the Shopify App Store (discussed below), Shopify released their Theme Store on April 20, 2010. The Theme Store offers free and paid themes for Shopify merchants.

"I remember the first time I saw Shopify and thinking wow, this is heck of a lot more elegant than Yahoo! Stores."
Eric Mueller, co-owner of Themepark

Your own storefront

Shopify provides the functionality necessary for individuals to build their own storefront to sell products from. Shopify customers can pick from over 50 free and premium themes from the Theme Store. Shopify has also released a product called Vision, which is a downloadable client application for designers to build and modify their own Shopify shop themes.

Manage your store

Shopify customers can manage and edit their store's content by logging into their Shopify administration account. They can edit their store's content, add new products, and accept payment from customers.

Shopify will also host the site on their fast servers and set up a **Secure Sockets Layer (SSL)**.

Accept payments

Shopify integrates with over 50 payment gateways, including Paypal, so any store can accept major credit cards within minutes of sign up.

They also support the sale of digital products through the Shopify App Fetch. Fetch is a digital delivery application that simplifies selling downloadable products.

Customers can also use drop shipping or fulfillment services, including Amazon Services, Shipwire, and Webgistix.

iPhone App

The online store can be run from an **iPhone or PDA using the Shopify application (App)**.

Shopify Analytics

Online analytics track and view store customers

Create promotions

Shopify stores can use Coupon codes, A/B testing, upload new banners and put products on sale.

Revenue Model

Creating a store is free. Shopify takes between a .05% - 2% commission on all sales. Shopify requires from its customers a valid Visa, MasterCard, American Express, or Discover card in order to process the payment

Set up fee	waived	waived	waived	waived	waived
Transaction Fee	2.0%	1.0%	1.0%	0.5%	0%
Max SKUs	100	2,500	10,000	25,000	50,000
Storage	100 MB	500 MB	1000 MB	2.54 GB	4.98 GB
Bandwidth	unlimited	unlimited	unlimited	unlimited	unlimited
Custom Domains	✔	✔	✔	✔	✔
SSL Checkout	✔	✔	✔	✔	✔
SSL Admin		✔	✔	✔	✔
Discount Codes		✔	✔	✔	✔
Carrier Shipping			✔	✔	✔
Real-Time Stats			✔	✔	✔
All prices are USD					

Figure 8: Shopify Fee Structure

With over 10,000 merchants currently using their product, Tobias, Aurélien and Harley had several opportunities and issues to discuss.

"What about changing our pricing model?" asked Harley, "Currently Shopify's customers are small to medium-sized companies. Should we start focusing on larger customers, after all some of our customers are now graduating and becoming bigger as well, some might leave us to go to our competitors, who are aimed at higher volume stores and have more features. Maybe we should even approach large well-established stores to handle their sites."

Tobias added "and some of our customers are dropping down in size and thus going to new smaller competitors of ours that offer lower prices with lower functionality, perhaps we should adjust our prices and functionality?"

Shopify had originally started offering its services for free with only a 3% commission. But as Aurélien recalled "That got us lots of people trying the software but only a small number of actual customers and studies have shown, that for companies offering a free basic level of service, for every 10 free customers they typically have only one paying customer."

"Should we offer more support", suggested Aurélien? In any service company, there is a need to support customers that who not only need to understand the service, but in Shopify's case, they might even need help in understanding the retail industry including how to market their stores. These two levels of service add to the cost of having a customer. Customers that require a great deal of assistance use up resources and might even become money losers for the company.

The company mission statement reads "At Shopify we strive to create amazing software while having as fun as possible. We all excel at solving complicated and meaningful challenges that affect thousands of businesses every day. Our customers use our products to create brilliant new businesses and we support them any way we can."

"Maybe we could have mentors" said Tobias, "Who could help customers with retail issues, for example, how to start a store, this could be an online seminar series or personal advisory service. What else could we provide?"

Tobias was also thinking about their next round of VC funding, as the company grew they would require more funding and thus would need to present a plan to investors, "maybe we should have another contest?" he mused out loud.

Harley quickly injected, "We could also build an apps store, in which our customers could add to the functionality of their site with apps that we or other third party vendors could supply. Do we have any predictions on whether our customers would use such apps?"

Aurélien asked, "How is the open source platform Ruby on Rails doing? Are we expecting new capabilities from that soon? Maybe we should switch to proprietary software as our technology platform?"

As the team thought about the issues, they knew Shopify had to take the next step but were unsure what that should be. They were confident that a solution would occur because their hiring processes had been aimed at fulfilling the mission statement; they had a company full of bright, energetic people who could solve problems.

Harley Finkelstein

Harley Finkelstein is a lawyer, entrepreneur, and the founder of one of Canada's leading promotional apparel companies. Additionally, Harley serves as a mentor to the Ottawa Centre for Research and Innovation (OCRI), sits on the financing committee for the Canadian Youth Business Foundation (CYBF), and is an advisor to both the Canadian Internet Policy and Public Interest Clinic (CIPPIC), and to the Ottawa Community Loan Fund (OCLF).

Harley received his law degree from the University of Ottawa, and completed his MBA at the school's management faculty. He is the co-founder of the school's Law/MBA Student Society, and the "Canadian MBA Oath". After graduating, Harley moved to Toronto to work for one of the city's leading business law firms, where he focused on corporate finance and commercial law.

Currently, Harley is the Chief Platform Officer (CPO) at Shopify, one of the web's leading eCommerce platforms.

James Bowen's biography is on page 44.

Aurélien Leftick

Aurélien Leftick makes Software as a Service (SaaS) addictive; ensuring that trial users converter into loyal paying customers. As the Director of Customer Success at Shopify, he was responsible for helping entrepreneurs create their online stores, get their first sale and ensure their continuous growth. He led initiatives such as the "Guru team" and the implementation of the gamification layer.

Prior to joining Shopify, Aurélien was an entrepreneur. He founded his first tech start-up in high school and received the OCRI Student Entrepreneur of the Year Award. After graduating from University of Ottawa, he joined PicSphere Technologies to help them raise funding and soon after became the company's CEO.

When not working, he is likely to be found among friends on a patio. He is online at leftick.com.

Judge's Notes on the Shopify case

Many entrepreneurial companies must deal with transitioning their company as they grow, signs of the need to change can include the changing customer segment from small unstable customers to large well-established customers. In that case, the issue is recognizing and preparing for the transition.

Currently Shopify is occupying a middle ground between the small and large ecommerce store providers. Customers who would use an online store creator package tend to enter the online retail market small and may grow in terms of volume and required functionality over time. Larger established stores might use commercially provided store provision tools but keep internal control over the site.

At a basic level this case is primarily focused on customer life cycle and sales funnel issues.

The issue is the retention rate of the customers. The contestants should recognize that a sales funnel has to be devised beginning with individual who doesn't even have a store and ending with store owners generating repeat online sales. As such Shopify needs to map each stage of the customers process and determine where the exit points are or problem areas and then determine if support, new pricing, new functionality, etc are needed for each stage. This also suggests the requirement for sales conversation metrics that reliably determine how many customers in each stage will convert to the next stage. It is this conversation and retention rate which needs to be measured and form the core of their support and sales organization strategy.

Another contest is probably not the best way to grow without first solving the sales funnel problem, and growth on to larger established retail outlets needs more direct sales support as larger stores will require support thus a better, more process-oriented organization will have to be established.

Contestants should really start with the mission statement which is too focused on having solutions to problems rather than setting up a system to allow Shopify's customers to grow. Contestants should really look to the necessary changes to transition the company to the next stage of its life cycle rather than merely deciding upon tactics.

Index

186

Titles published by Invenire Books

10. Michael Behiels & François Rocher (eds)   2011
    The State in Transition: Challenges for Canadian Federalism

9. Pierre Camu   2011
    La flotte blanche : Histoire de la companie de navigation du Richelieu et d'Ontario

8. Rupak Chattopadhyay & Gilles Paquet (eds)   2011
    The Unimagined Canadian Capital: Challenges for the Federal Capital Region

7. Gilles Paquet   2011
    Tableau d'avancement II : Essais exploratoires sur la gouvernance d'un certain Canada français

6. James Bowen (ed) 2011
    The Entrepreneurial Effect: Waterloo

5. François Lapointe   2011
    Cities as Crucibles: Reflections on Canada's Urban Future

4. James Bowen (ed)   2009
    The Entrepreneurial Effect (Ottawa entrepreneurs)

3. Gilles Paquet   2009
    Scheming Virtuously: the road to collaborative governance

2. Ruth Hubbard   2009
    Profession: Public Servant

1. Robin Higham   2009
    Who do we think we are: Canada's reasonable (and less reasonable) accommodation debates